The Unofficial TikTok Drink Recipe Book

100+ Internet-Breaking Recipes for Coffees, Milkshakes, Mocktails, Cocktails, and More!

Palestrina McCaffrey @littleremyfood

ADAMS MEDIA
NEW YORK AMSTERDAM/ANTWERP LONDON
TORONTO SYDNEY/MELBOURNE NEW DELHI

A adamsmedia

Adams Media
An Imprint of Simon & Schuster, LLC
100 Technology Center Drive
Stoughton, MA 02072

First Adams Media hardcover edition September 2026

ADAMS MEDIA and colophon are registered trademarks of Simon & Schuster, LLC.

Simon & Schuster strongly believes in freedom of expression and stands against censorship in all its forms. For more information, visit BooksBelong.com.

For information about special discounts for bulk purchases, please contact Simon & Schuster Special Sales at 1-866-506-1949 or business@simonandschuster.com.

The Simon & Schuster Speakers Bureau can bring authors to your live event. For more information or to book an event, contact the Simon & Schuster Speakers Bureau at 1-866-248-3049 or visit our website at www.simonspeakers.com.

Interior design by Erin Alexander
Illustrations by Priscilla Yuen
Photographs by Harper Point Photography
Photographer: Nathan Rega
Food stylist and chef: Kira Friedman
Author photo by Marc Cartwright Photography

Manufactured in China

10 9 8 7 6 5 4 3 2 1

Library of Congress Cataloging-in-Publication Data has been applied for.

ISBN 978-1-5072-2629-2
ISBN 978-1-5072-2630-8 (ebook)

Contents

CHAPTER 3

Energy Boosting & Hydration / 45

CHAPTER 4

Sodas & Sparkling Beverages / 71

CHAPTER 5

Frozen & Dessert Drinks / 95

CHAPTER 6

Entertaining / 121

CHAPTER 7

Mocktails & Cocktails / 153

Introduction

Cracked Dubai Chocolate Milkshakes . . . Pineapple Whip Floats . . . Cotton Candy Margaritas . . . 🥰

If there's one thing TikTok knows, it's how to turn a beverage into a full-on *moment*. From a color-changing combo of ingredients, an oh-so-satisfying clink of ice cubes into a garnished glass, or an over-load of indulgent flavors, #DrinkTok has taken over your FYP, one satisfying swirl at a time.

And now these drool-worthy drinks can be made right at home!

The Unofficial TikTok Drink Recipe Book is your behind-the-scenes pass for re-creating the most talked about trends. Inside, you'll find 110(!!) easy DIYs inspired by TikTok's most viral sips, from Cloud Coffee and Dragon Fruit Hwachae to Jelly Soda and Froot Loops Shots. Even better, there's no barista training required, no hard-to-find ingredients, and no intimidating equipment to clutter your counter.

Organized into chapters from specialty coffees to sippable desserts to fun shareables and more, this collection is designed to match whatever vibe you're chasing. Need a morning pick-me-up? There's a Honeycomb Latte for that. Hosting friends? The color-changing Butterfly Pea Flower Tea Lemonade is *guaranteed* to impress. Looking for a sweet treat? Sink into a luxe Thin Mint Frosted Shake. Whatever you're craving, scroll no further because your next obsession is already here. 😋

You'll also discover a chapter full of tips for making TikTok's top hits (and spotting recipes that aren't worth the hype). Plus you'll get insider guidance on what basic tools and ingredients to keep on hand as you start re-creating viral beverages at home.

Whether you love a tasty trend, are into curating the perfect aesthetic, or just want to try something new, this book is here to help you turn saved videos into real-life favorites. So grab your favorite glass, turn up the vibes, and let's get mixing!

CHAPTER 1

The Essentials of TikTok Drinks

Scrolling TikTok, drinks are *everywhere*. From iced coffees layered with impossibly thick (and tasty) foams to lemonades that change color as you pour them, #DrinkTok has turned plain old beverages into something you just *have* to stop and stare at. They aren't just drool-worthy—they're ✨ aesthetic ✨ TikTok's viral drinks are made to be shared!

But why are some drinks all over your FYP while others never seem to have their moment? Is it the look? The flavor? How easy (or not so easy) they are to make at home? And more importantly, what do you need to re-create these drinks yourself—without investing in an over-the-top setup? This chapter is here to help!

You'll learn which tools will help you tackle any recipe, which ingredients you'll need to whip up a ton of trends, and how to know when a popular drink is worth your time—or not. From quick refreshers to indulgent shakes, understanding these basics will make checking out the hype (and experimenting with your own twists!) a whole lot of fun. Before you start shaking, stirring, and layering, consider this your starting point. Ready to bring TikTok's top hits to your own kitchen? Let's jump in!

#DrinkTok

Not all that long ago, fancy-looking (and tasting) drinks felt like something you just ordered somewhere—not something you made. Special coffees like dessert-flavored lattes came from cafés, flashy cocktails with edible glitter came from bars, and all the little details behind them stayed mostly behind the counter. If you loved a drink, you could ask how it was made, but the answer might be vague, *if* you got an answer at all.

#DrinkTok changed all that. Instead of gatekeeping yummy recipes, people began not just making drinks for online audiences but breaking it down step-by-step, showing exact measurements, techniques, and shortcuts that anyone could follow. Baristas started sharing café tricks, bartenders gave away the secrets of classic cocktails, and home creators proved you don't need professional training to make something delicious *and* impressive. Viral DIYs focused on short ingredient lists, easy-to-find tools, and beginner-friendly steps. And suddenly, making great drinks became accessible to everyone. 🥰

What really makes #DrinkTok such a hit, though, is how quickly the ideas travel. One person posts a drink. Someone else re-creates it. Another adds a twist (like swapping flavors, changing the texture, or leveling up the presentation). Each version builds on the last, and before long, a single idea turns into a full-blown trend that has people saying, "OMG I need to try that!" That shared energy is what makes #DrinkTok feel less like a bunch of recipes online and more like a collaborative DIY.

#Trending Sips

POV: You're scrolling TikTok when suddenly something catches your eye and makes you stop. Maybe it's a slow pour, a dramatic color change, or a texture you can't quite place. You don't even know what the drink is yet, but you're hooked! That moment is where most of the biggest trends begin.

Now, the same drink is showing up again—and each time, it's slightly different from the last one you saw. One version is simple, another is all dressed up, and others add a special twist that pushes the OG further. Suddenly, that drink isn't just a recipe; it's a trending convo. Not only are you watching how it's made, you're watching how people react to it, adjust it, and make it their own. You may even be hearing about it outside of your social feeds too!

What keeps certain drinks on everyone's radar isn't just how often they pop up online; it's the surprise that each recipe offers. Many of the most talked-about sips introduce something unexpected: layered colors that stay perfectly separated, foams that float effortlessly on top, or flavors that seem like they *shouldn't* work but somehow do. Popular drinks challenge what a beverage is *supposed* to look or taste like.

At the same time, the things you *do* already know and love play a role. Some trends remix classic faves, giving them a fresh format or updated presentation (check out the Dirty Shirley Temple or Raspberry Lime Mojito). Others feel bold because they bend traditional rules *just* enough to feel new without being intimidating. Add in the shareability factor (hello, hashtags!), and you've got the perfect recipe for something blowing up online. The more a drink makes people stop, watch, and wonder, the longer it sticks around on TikTok—and beyond.

Worth the Hype . . . or Not?

Not *every* viral drink deserves a spot in your glass, though. Some trends take off because they're easy to love and easy to make. Others get some hype because they look awesome on camera . . . even if the flavor doesn't quite live up to the moment, or the instructions are super involved or confusing. Knowing the difference between what is worth a try and what isn't saves time, ingredients, and plain old disappointment.

Luckily, a drink that isn't worth the hype is going to have a red flag or two that make it easier to spot. And before running to your kitchen to whip up a hit recipe, it helps to keep an eye out for them. Paying attention not just to how a drink looks on your FYP but how it's being made, what's said about it, and more can tell you *a lot* before you ever pick up a shaker.

Here are a few tips for figuring out whether a drink is worth trying:

- **Consider the effort involved.** A long ingredient list or complicated prep doesn't always mean a better drink.
- **Look beyond the visuals.** If the appeal relies entirely on color, foam, or a single trick, the flavor may be an afterthought (IOW, not great).
- **Notice how often it's re-created.** Drinks that people return to, rather than just try once, tend to be the best.
- **Watch the reactions closely.** Genuine enjoyment is hard to fake. If creators keep sipping and singing its praises, that's a good sign!

Ultimately, the best trends are the ones that earn a repeat pour—not just by creators but by *you*! Trust your instincts, skip what doesn't excite you, and *don't* feel obligated to chase every viral moment.

When a drink fits *your* taste, *your* time, and *your* aesthetic, the hype takes care of itself. 😋

Essential Tools for Viral Drinks

Viral drinks might look complicated, but TikTok has a way of making every recipe feel high effort, when in reality, many hits are built on simplicity. So most of them use the same short list of tools for different needs. You may have already spotted some of them across coffee drinks, mocktails, cocktails, refreshers, and more—sometimes doing the same job, sometimes doing something completely unexpected. Here are the go-tos you'll wanna have in your own kitchen:

- **Blender.** From frozen lemonades to slushy cocktails and smoothie-style drinks, a blender opens the door to an entirely different category of viral sips. Many drinks use crushed ice or frozen textures, and a blender makes these possible in seconds.
- **Cocktail shaker or sealed jar.** Shaking chills, blends, and slightly dilutes drinks for better balance. Whether you're working with citrus, syrups, or spirits, a shaker (or even a tightly sealed jar!) helps bring everything together quickly and evenly.
- **Fine mesh strainer.** Essential for smooth pours, especially when you're dealing with fruit pulp, herbs, or foam.
- **Handheld frother.** This is one of the most used tools on #DrinkTok for a reason. Frothers are responsible for whipped coffee, cold foam, mixed powders, and airy toppings that instantly elevate a drink. Small, affordable, and easy to use, a frother is often the difference between a flat drink and one that is absolute 🔥

- **Ice trays and molds.** Clear cubes, crushed ice, spheres—ice isn't just functional; it's part of the presentation! Different drinks shine with different ice styles and can completely change the way a recipe looks and feels.
- **Jigger or measuring cups.** Consistency matters, especially when a drink is meant to be re-created. Measuring ensures balance and helps you tweak recipes with confidence instead of guesswork.
- **Muddler.** Fresh fruits, herbs, and spices show up on #DrinkTok more than you might expect. A muddler helps release their flavors without overworking the ingredients, making it an essential tool for minty refreshers, citrus-forward mocktails, layered flavor builds, and more.
- **Tall glasses and clear cups.** Layered colors, textures, and foams deserve to be shown off in clear glasses.

You don't need a full bar setup to make TikTok-worthy drinks. Once the above essentials are in place, experimenting with new hits becomes easier—and a lot more fun!

Must-Have Drink Staples

Viral drinks don't require a shelf full of special ingredients with fancy names, but they *do* rely on a few smart staples that can be mixed, layered, and adapted across countless TikTok faves. These are the ingredients that quietly show up again and again on you FYP, forming the base of everything from refreshing mocktails to café-style faves. In addition to the tools discussed, here are the ingredients you should keep on hand:

- **Citrus.** Lemons, limes, and oranges add brightness and structure. Fresh citrus is especially important in popular drinks that rely on contrast to cut through sweetness, enhance aroma, and keep flavors from feeling flat.
- **Coffee and tea bases.** Espresso, cold brew, matcha, and brewed teas form the backbone of many #DrinkTok creations. Ready-made or instant espresso is particularly useful for quick sips, iced drinks, and recipes that don't require a full espresso machine.
- **Flavor enhancers.** Vanilla extract, flavored syrups, fruit purées, and spices like cinnamon help fine-tune a drink. And small amounts go a *looong* way, making these some of the most powerful ingredients to have.
- **Fresh herbs.** Mint shows up constantly in popular drinks for good reason. Keeping a mint plant on hand ensures better flavor, stronger aroma, and easy access whenever a recipe calls for a bright, herbal finish.
- **Milk and milk alternatives.** Whole milk, heavy cream, oat milk, almond milk, and similar options are essential for lattes, foams, and creamy textures. Different milks behave differently when frothed or shaken, making them a simple way to customize drinks.
- **Sparkling water and sodas.** Fizz adds refreshing fun to a drink. These are key for mocktails, spritz-style drinks, and lighter variations of richer recipes.
- **Sweeteners.** Granulated sugar, brown sugar, honey, and simple syrup are a *must* for balance. They soften acidity, support flavor, and adapt easily to hot or cold drinks. Having more than one option for a sweetener lets you adjust depth and sweetness without changing the overall recipe.

With these staples, you'll be able to re-create so many viral drinks without last-minute grocery runs. More importantly, you'll be able to adjust, experiment, and build drinks that suit *your* tastes and not just the current craze.

Bringing #DrinkTok to Your Glass

Making TikTok drinks at home isn't about getting everything perfect, but trying things out and having fun through the process. Some drinks will come together easily, while others may need a small adjustment or a second try. It's all part of the experience! Viral drinks work best when you treat them as starting points, not strict instructions. Once you understand how flavors balance and textures are created, you can tweak recipes for what you're craving instead of chasing exact replicas.

It's also worth remembering that what you see online is usually the polished result of trial and error. That perfect layering effect could have taken the creator a few attempts—or ten! That amazing pairing of flavors might have involved some back-and-forth to get the measurements right. As you dig into the recipes ahead, think of them as delicious invites to experiment. Try them as written, then make them your own. With the solid foundation provided in this chapter, bringing the best blends to your own glass becomes a tasty adventure! 🥰

CHAPTER 2

Coffees & Lattes

Pumpkin Spiced Latte

The most iconic drink of fall: the Pumpkin Spiced Latte This is *the* drink that mixes warm, sweet vibes with a heart of delightful holiday. With its creaminess, cinnamon, and velvety texture, it'll keep you oh so cozy through sweater weather season.

SERVES 1

2 tablespoons pumpkin purée

½ teaspoon pumpkin spice blend (cinnamon, ginger, cloves, nutmeg, ground black pepper)

1 tablespoon maple syrup

1 teaspoon vanilla extract

1 tablespoon packed dark brown sugar

1 cup whole milk

2 ounces espresso

Canned whipped cream

Ground cinnamon

1. In a small saucepan over medium heat, stir together pumpkin purée and pumpkin spice blend. Add maple syrup, vanilla, and sugar. Cook 2–3 minutes, stirring constantly, until mixture slightly caramelizes and becomes a thick syrup.
2. Slowly add milk and cook 3–4 minutes, stirring until mixture almost starts to boil. Remove from heat and stir in espresso.
3. Pour into a glass mug and top with whipped cream. Sprinkle a little cinnamon on top and enjoy!

#ForYou Tips

Feeling extra fancy? You can hollow out a small pumpkin and pour this drink into it for extra fun fall vibes!

Iced White Mocha

When a drink goes viral, there's always a rush to re-create it at home just like the picture on your phone. Which is why this Iced White Mocha got attention! This creamy, delectable drink is the perfect excuse to try an in-store staple for yourself. Chocolatey goodness meets coffee blend, topped off with cold whole milk—it's the most irresistible way to start off any morning.

SERVES 1

2 ounces espresso
1 tablespoon white chocolate sauce
1 cup whole milk
Canned whipped cream

1. In a tall glass filled with ice, mix espresso and white chocolate sauce together.
2. Pour milk into glass and stir until combined. Top with whipped cream and enjoy!

Pistachio Chocolate Latte

The perfect combo of chocolate and pistachio has been megaviral since Dubai chocolate took center stage. It's about time a latte version came around! This Pistachio Chocolate Latte is the upgrade you didn't know you needed in your life. With its signature greenish tint and a whole lot of creamy goodness all in one cup, you'll be drinking this one every season.

SERVES 1

1½ cups whole milk

2 ounces semisweet baking chocolate, finely chopped, plus more for optional shaving garnish

1 tablespoon pistachio paste

1 ounce espresso

Canned whipped cream

1. In a small saucepan over medium heat, heat milk 5–10 minutes until boiling, stirring constantly. Once boiling, reduce heat to a low simmer and add in chocolate and pistachio paste. Slowly stir until completely combined, about 5 minutes.
2. In a mug, add espresso followed by milk mixture. Mix well. Top with whipped cream and chocolate shavings if you fancy them!

#ForYou Tips

Give it an extra indulgent twist by replacing the chocolate with Nutella hazelnut spread for a nuttier flavor.

Iced Strawberry Matcha Latte

When it comes to satisfying drinks, this Iced Strawberry Matcha Latte hits the spot! It's a refreshing combo of creaminess, strawberries, and matcha. Plus the colors are so irresistible. What started as a go-to drive-through order has turned into an easy DIY that you can sip on any day.

SERVES 1

¼ cup finely chopped fresh strawberries

1 tablespoon granulated sugar

1 teaspoon matcha powder

2 tablespoons hot water

¾ cup whole milk

1. In a tall glass, add strawberries and sugar. Muddle until you get a thick syrup consistency. Set aside.
2. In a small bowl, add matcha powder and water and whisk vigorously until frothy and smooth. Set aside.
3. Add some ice and milk to strawberry mixture, leaving room at the top. Top with matcha. Slowly stir to combine and serve.

Honeycomb Latte

Honeycomb candy has taken off online for its crunchy, caramelized taste. Now in drink form, the Honeycomb Latte is deliciously sweet and cozy, with a little crunch on top for a supersatisfying experience. It's the perfect cozy morning pick-me-up! 🥰

SERVES 1

¼ cup granulated sugar
5 teaspoons water
1½ teaspoons baking soda
1 ounce espresso
½ tablespoon honey
1 cup whole milk

1. In a medium heatproof bowl, mix sugar and water together, and microwave 3 minutes, until sugar is caramelized. Make sure to check on it every 30 seconds or so.
2. Pour sugar mixture into a parchment-lined mug and add baking soda, stirring until fully combined. The honeycomb should expand in the dish. Let it cool at least 25 minutes.
3. Once cooled, remove parchment paper and crush honeycomb into smaller sizes.
4. In a tall glass filled with ice, add espresso, honey, and milk. Mix together well. (You can also use a frother to blend these ingredients before adding ice. Be careful not to make it too frothy.) Place honeycomb pieces on top.

#ForYou Tips

If there's too much or not enough air in your honeycomb, you can adjust the baking soda amount. Add more baking soda for more air, or less baking soda for less air. The final candy should have bubbles and taste sweet. 😋

Tahini Coffee

Sometimes the unexpected gets a name for itself—just like this Tahini Coffee! This one went viral for its sweet, nutty flavors and unexpected ingredient. Surprising and delicious, tahini is a ground paste made from toasted sesame seeds, kind of like peanut butter.

SERVES 1

1 tablespoon tahini
1 tablespoon maple syrup
1 cup whole milk
⅛ teaspoon salt
1 ounce espresso
Ground cinnamon

1. In a small saucepan over medium heat, heat tahini, maple syrup, and milk until just before boiling. Reduce heat to low, add salt, and simmer 2 minutes.
2. Pour mixture into a glass mug and then add espresso. Top with cinnamon. Enjoy!

Whipped Dalgona

Whipped Dalgona has a major following online—you can't miss it! Originating in Korea, Whipped Dalgona is made by blending equal parts coffee, water, and sugar so it foams up into a light fluffy cloud of cold brew. Absolutely delicious, and especially great for those work-from-home vibes!

SERVES 1

2 tablespoons instant coffee
2 tablespoons granulated sugar
2 tablespoons hot water
¾ cup whole milk

1. In a small bowl, combine coffee, sugar, and water. Using a frother, blend until mixture is creamy, bubbly, and lightens in color, about 3–4 minutes.
2. Fill a mug or glass with ice and then add milk. Gently spoon coffee mixture on top. Serve and enjoy!

Dirty Chai Latte

There's no denying that chai is one of the most popular drinks out there, but this Dirty Chai Latte turns things up a notch. Warm, sweet, and spiced, it's the coziest drink. You'll wanna make it again and again!

SERVES 1

¾ cup whole milk

3 tablespoons TAZO Classic Chai Latte Tea Concentrate

2 teaspoons honey

2 ounces espresso

In a small saucepan over medium-low, heat milk, chai, and honey. Let simmer 2 minutes. Once heated, pour into a mug. Add in espresso, stir, and serve.

Banana Cold Foam Coffee

Bananas are one of those foods where you can end up with a bunch—and not enough time (or ideas) to use them all. But thanks to this Banana Cold Foam Coffee, it'll be so easy to use any extras for something absolutely yummy. This drink is like an elegant bananas Foster in a glass, all caramelized and delicious with every sip.

SERVES 1

½ medium ripe banana, plus 3 slices for garnish

3 tablespoons heavy whipping cream

1 teaspoon maple syrup

⅛ teaspoon vanilla extract

1 ounce blonde espresso

¾ cup whole milk

Ground cinnamon

1. In a cup, muddle banana into a fine paste. Pour in cream, maple syrup, and vanilla. Froth 1–2 minutes until creamy and a foam has formed.
2. In a tall glass filled with ice, add espresso and milk. Mix and top with cold foam. Garnish with a sprinkle of cinnamon and 3 banana slices. Enjoy!

Cracked Matcha Latte

Cracked lattes aren't just fun to drink, they have one of *the* most satisfying ASMR sounds. Every sip and bite of a Cracked Matcha Latte is a little different and totally immersive.

SERVES 2

2 (4-ounce) bars semisweet baking chocolate, chopped

2 teaspoons matcha powder

¼ cup hot water

2 cups whole milk

1 tablespoon honey

1. Over medium-low heat, place chocolate in the top of a double boiler or a heatproof bowl set over a pot of simmering water. Stir constantly until melted, about 5–10 minutes, being careful not to let the temperature exceed 90°F, then remove from heat.
2. Pour melted chocolate into a 16-ounce clear, flexible plastic cup and carefully swirl it around, tapping the cup until it's fully coated. Pour remaining chocolate back into the bowl. Repeat with a second cup.
3. Freeze chocolate cups 3 minutes or until chocolate is solid.
4. In a small bowl, add matcha powder and water. Whisk until smooth and foamy. Set aside.
5. In a small saucepan over medium-high heat, heat milk about 5 minutes to a slight boil. Reduce heat to low and add matcha mixture and honey. Whisk until matcha powder dissolves completely, about 2 minutes. Remove from heat and refrigerate at least 15 minutes until cool.
6. In the chocolate-coated cups, add ice and pour matcha mixture over top. Squeeze the cups to crack the chocolate shells and serve.

Cloud Coffee

TikTok is always finding fun ways to make a morning coffee more interesting, like this sweet little mix. Cloud Coffee features the popular dalgona coffee floating on top of clear coconut water to make it look like an edible cloud in the sky. This drink is deliciously creamy and brewed to perfection, with subtle notes from the honey and coconut water. You'll be excited to get up and drink this every day of the week!

SERVES 1

2 tablespoons instant coffee

2 tablespoons honey

2 tablespoons hot water

¾ cup coconut water

1. In a small bowl, combine coffee, honey, and hot water. Using a frother, blend until mixture is creamy, bubbly, and lightens in color, about 3–4 minutes.
2. Fill a tall glass with ice and then add coconut water. Float coffee mixture on top.

Avocado Latte

Move over, avocado toast—the Avocado Latte is the talk of breakfast delight! That's right, Avocado *Latte*. Hear it out: Avocado might sound weird for a coffee drink, but it's not just viral for the novel flavor and fun (some people are serving it up in an actual avocado!). The avocado makes the drink smooth and creamy, with just the right amount of sweetness to bring you back for a second cup . . . or a third 😋

SERVES 1

1 medium avocado, peeled and pitted

1 tablespoon honey

1 cup whole milk

1 ounce espresso

1. Add avocado into a small bowl and mash until as smooth as possible. Add honey and mix well.
2. Pour in milk and mix until incorporated. Then blend with a frother until creamy.
3. Pour into a tall glass, then add espresso. Top with a little ice.

#ForYou Tips

🔥 **Make sipping even more aesthetic by pouring this drink into a large hollowed-out avocado peel. To avoid spilling, place the avocado peel inside a round cookie cutter before you pour.**

Viral NYC Hot Chocolate

New York just doesn't miss! This iconic, viral hot chocolate is known for a marshmallow overload that no one can resist. Every sip so angelic you'll be craving more.

SERVES 2

½ cup heavy whipping cream
1 teaspoon vanilla extract
1 teaspoon confectioners' sugar
1½ cups whole milk
2 (4-ounce) bars semisweet baking chocolate, finely chopped
½ teaspoon ground cinnamon
⅛ teaspoon ground nutmeg
½ cup Marshmallow Fluff

1. In the bowl of an electric mixer, beat cream, vanilla, and sugar until stiff peaks form, about 2 minutes. Set aside.
2. In a small saucepan over medium-high heat, heat milk to a simmer, about 2 minutes. Reduce heat to low and whisk in chocolate, cinnamon, and nutmeg.
3. Thickly coat the rims of two heatproof glasses with Fluff (you can use a piping bag to help). Using a blowtorch, carefully toast Fluff to a brownish color but not burnt.
4. Pour hot chocolate into the prepared glasses and top each with a dollop of whipped cream. Serve and enjoy!

Matcha Hot Chocolate

Want a little more than OG hot chocolate? This Matcha Hot Chocolate is the perfect thing! It doesn't just taste creamy and comforting but also has all that matcha flavoring. It's perfect for those cozy by the fire vibes.

SERVES 1

1½ cups whole milk

1 (4-ounce) bar white baking chocolate, finely chopped

2 teaspoons matcha powder

½ teaspoon hot water

Canned whipped cream

1. In a small saucepan over medium heat, heat milk until simmering, about 3 minutes. Reduce heat to medium-low and carefully add chocolate. Whisk until completely melted. Set aside.
2. In a small bowl, whisk matcha powder and water until matcha blooms (tiny bubbles form on the surface), about 2 minutes.
3. Pour matcha into chocolate mixture and stir well.
4. Pour into a mug and top with whipped cream. Enjoy!

#ForYou Tips

To be extra fancy, you can shave white chocolate over top of the hot chocolate and sprinkle a little matcha powder over the shavings!

Teddy Bear Latte

Everybody loves the classic throwback flavor of Teddy Grahams, which is why this latte went viral. The Teddy Bear Latte is a delicious honey and cinnamon combo in a glass. Topped with a little extra spice and some extra Teddy Grahams, it's gonna hit the spot.

SERVES 1

1 tablespoon honey

1 tablespoon crushed Teddy Grahams, divided

¼ teaspoon ground cinnamon, plus more for garnish

1–2 ounces espresso

1 cup whole milk

2–3 whole Teddy Grahams

1. In a glass or mug, combine honey, ½ tablespoon crushed Teddy Grahams, and cinnamon. Mix well.
2. Pour in espresso, some ice, and milk and stir. Carefully add remaining crushed and whole Teddy Grahams on top. Sprinkle with a little more cinnamon and serve.

Cookie Butter Latte

When the Internet decides certain flavors are *it*, it's not messing around. This cold Cookie Butter Latte has gotten attention thanks to the Biscoff creamy cookie butter spread that went viral. The sweet, crispy Biscoff cookie is now even better because you can satisfy your craving without waiting for dessert.

SERVES 1

¼ cup heavy whipping cream

1 tablespoon plus 1½ teaspoons Biscoff creamy cookie butter spread, divided

1 ounce espresso

½ cup whole milk

2 Biscoff cookies, divided

1. In a small glass, make cold foam: Add cream and ½ teaspoon cookie butter and blend with a frother. Set aside.
2. In a small cup or bowl, add 1 tablespoon cookie butter and espresso. Mix well and set aside.
3. Assemble: Swirl the inside of a tall glass or 16-ounce plastic cup with remaining 1 teaspoon cookie butter and fill with ice. Pour espresso mixture and milk over ice, leaving room at the top, and stir gently.
4. Carefully pour in cold foam over the top of the drink. Crumble 1 cookie over the top and garnish with remaining whole cookie. Enjoy!

2CUP

Tiramisu Latte

People have been turning everything into a take on tiramisu: bathtubs, desk drawers, and even claw machines. So of course the Tiramisu Latte was next in line! This delectable drink is creamy, sweet, and *sooo* worth the hype. Each layer blends perfectly with the last for a rich, decadent vibe, and the drink itself melts in your mouth.

SERVES 1

¼ cup heavy whipping cream
1 teaspoon vanilla extract
2 tablespoons mascarpone
1 tablespoon maple syrup
1 ounce espresso
½ teaspoon cocoa powder, plus more for garnish
½ teaspoon packed dark brown sugar
½ cup whole milk
1 ladyfinger

1. In a tall glass or measuring cup, mix cream, vanilla, mascarpone, and maple syrup. With a frother, blend mixture until it becomes a creamy cold foam. Set aside.
2. In a small glass, stir together espresso, cocoa, and sugar until well mixed.
3. In another tall glass or 16-ounce clear plastic cup, pour in milk and blend with a frother until creamy. Fill glass halfway with ice. Slowly add espresso mixture to create a layer on top, then slowly add cream mixture for the final layer.
4. Sprinkle with cocoa and garnish with a ladyfinger. Enjoy!

Nutella Whipped Coffee

Not much is more popular than the sugary deliciousness of Nutella, and this Nutella Whipped Coffee is a morning must! Brewed with all those hazelnut flavors, this cold, creamy drink is *sooo* indulgent. It's based on the viral dalgona coffee but with a couple twists to make it even *more* irresistible. It's one favorite that definitely lives up to the hype!

SERVES 1

1 cup whole milk

3 tablespoons Nutella hazelnut spread

2 tablespoons instant coffee

2 tablespoons granulated sugar

2 tablespoons hot water

1. In a small saucepan over medium-low heat, heat milk to a simmer, about 2 minutes. Add in Nutella and stir until completely combined. Remove from heat and set aside.
2. In a small bowl, combine coffee, sugar, and water. Using a frother, blend until mixture is creamy, bubbly, and lightens in color, about 3–4 minutes.
3. Pour Nutella milk into a mug and top with coffee mixture. Enjoy!

CHAPTER 3

Energy Boosting & Hydration

Deli Container Refresher

Move over, cucumber water: Fruit refreshers are now in TikTok season! These drinks went viral for good reason: They are the perfect blend of delicious fruity flavors. The best thing about this trend is that you can make them any way you like. Just add water and fruit, and you've mastered the Deli Container Refresher!

SERVES 1

6 fresh mint leaves
¼ cup fresh blueberries
¼ cup chopped fresh strawberries
2 tablespoons fresh blackberries
½ medium orange, cut into wedges
1 medium lemon, cut into wedges
1–2 tablespoons granulated sugar
½ cup coconut water
1 cup cold water

1. Place mint, blueberries, strawberries, blackberries, orange wedges, lemon wedges, and sugar in a 32-ounce deli container. Muddle until all fruits release their juices.
2. Add coconut water, cold water, and some ice. Put the lid on the container and shake until well combined. Punch the container with a straw and enjoy!

#ForYou Tips

You can replace cold water with sparkling water for a bubbly twist.

Almost a Pink Drink

The Starbucks Pink Drink has become one of the most ✨ iconic ✨ drinks on TikTok. This mixed berry drink is creamy, colorful, and an ultimate dream for your taste buds. Better than any ordinary refresher, it's got people asking, "What's actually in it?!" And now, thanks to this easy take on the OG, you can enjoy those luscious flavors right at home.

SERVES 1

¼ cup fresh or frozen strawberries
1 mixed berry tea bag
½ cup hot water
1 cup unsweetened coconut milk
1 tablespoon honey
2 tablespoons lemon juice
¼ cup freeze-dried strawberries

1. Add fresh or frozen strawberries to a blender and blend until completely smooth. Strain strawberry juice into a bowl. Set aside.
2. Steep tea bag in hot water, cool, then add to strawberry juice. Add tea, coconut milk, honey, and lemon juice. Stir until completely combined.
3. Fill a tall glass or 16-ounce clear plastic cup with ice and pour in strawberry mixture. Top with freeze-dried strawberries. Serve and enjoy!

Nature's Gatorade

Registered dietitian Ashley Koff was quoted calling coconut water Nature's Gatorade back in 2009, and the name has since been used to describe a wide range of coconut water–based drink recipes trending all over the Internet. The naturally infused fruity flavors in this version lets you skip the artificial dyes and focus on pure ingredients and staying hydrated!

SERVES 1

2 cups cubed watermelon
¼ cup fresh strawberries
2 medium lemons, juiced
1 medium lime, juiced
1½ cups coconut water
⅛ teaspoon salt
2 tablespoons honey

1. In a blender, blend watermelon and strawberries until smooth. Strain mixture and pour into a large glass.
2. Add lemon juice, lime juice, coconut water, salt, and honey to glass. Stir well and enjoy!

#ForYou Tips

For different colors and flavors, mix and match different fruit blends like honeydew, cantaloupe, pineapple, or oranges.

Citrus Loaded Water

Spa water, take a back seat. Citrus Loaded Water is the new GOAT of the Internet. This drink is quick to make and doesn't skip on flavor. Full of natural ingredients and electrolytes, it'll keep you quenched the whole day. It's a supertasty break from sugary drinks—without skipping the hydration.

SERVES 2

2 cups water

1 (0.2-ounce) packet lemon electrolyte drink mix (like LMNT or Liquid IV)

2 medium lemons, juiced

1 medium lime, juiced

½ medium grapefruit, juiced

2 medium oranges, juiced

1 wheel each lemon, lime, grapefruit, and orange

1. In a large glass, add water and electrolyte mix and stir to combine.
2. Add fruit juices. Fill halfway with ice and garnish with citrus wheels.

#ForYou Tips

To switch up the flavors, you can try different refreshing fruits and electrolyte packets. Try mango, watermelon, or berry.

Viral Ocean Water Lemonade

Deli containers got themselves an upgrade thanks to this Viral Ocean Water Lemonade. It perfectly combines the sweet flavor of coconut with sour lemons. Just shake, stab a straw, and you've got yourself the best drink of the summer (or anytime the craving hits)!

SERVES 1

1 medium lemon, cut into wedges
2 tablespoons granulated sugar
½ tablespoon coconut syrup
½ tablespoon blue raspberry syrup
1 tablespoon pineapple juice
1 cup blue Powerade
1 cup Sprite soda

1. In a 32-ounce clear deli container, add lemon wedges and sugar. Muddle until all lemon juice is released.
2. Add coconut syrup, blue raspberry syrup, pineapple juice, and Powerade. Fill container with ice, leaving some room at the top, cover with a lid, and shake it up.
3. Open the lid and top off with Sprite. Place the lid back on tightly, punch the container with a straw, and enjoy!

Watermelon Agua Fresca

Watermelon is a fruit fave when it comes to summertime. . . . Now match that with agua fresca? Genuine melt! This drink doesn't only highlight the sweet, juicy watermelon but also creates a balanced, refreshing mint and lime flavor. There's no wonder it went viral!

SERVES 3

3 cups cubed watermelon
2 medium limes, cut into wedges
15 fresh mint leaves
⅛ cup granulated sugar (optional)
⅛ cup Tajín seasoning
3 lime wheels

1. Place watermelon into a blender and blend until completely smooth. Strain watermelon juice into a pitcher.
2. Place lime wedges and mint in a medium bowl. Muddle until all juice is out of limes and mint is broken down and incorporated.
3. Add lime mixture to watermelon mixture and stir to combine. If desired, add sugar, a little at a time, until it's as sweet as you like. Strain agua fresca one more time into a clean pitcher.
4. Sprinkle Tajín on a clean plate. Carefully wet the top of three tall glasses and press the rims into Tajín. Pour agua fresca into glasses and top each with a lime wheel. Enjoy!

#ForYou Tips

This drink is just as good without the sugar—or with more if you like things even sweeter! Just adjust the amount to whatever you like.

Southern Sweet Tea

This unique twist on the OG Southern classic is *made* for hydration. With light tastes of lemon and black iced tea, it's a supercozy drink that's trending for good reason 🔥

SERVES 3

3 cups water
6 black tea bags
½ cup granulated sugar
½ medium lemon, sliced

1. Add water to a small pot over high heat and boil. Once boiling, add tea bags and steep 5 minutes. Add sugar and mix until completely dissolved.
2. Pour into a pitcher and refrigerate until cooled (at least 4 hours, up to overnight).
3. Serve in tall glasses filled with ice and garnish with lemon slices.

#ForYou Tips

If you don't like black tea, you can replace it with an iced tea drink mix from the store. 😋

Refreshing Strawberry Acai

Popularized by a beloved coffee chain, refreshers like the Strawberry Acai have become one of the Internet's favorite drinks when it comes to staying cool. And this twist on the fan fave is *not* one to miss. It's deliciously icy, sweet, and sour—and, best of all, easy to make at home!

SERVES 1

2 tablespoons freeze-dried strawberry powder

1 teaspoon acai powder

4–8 tablespoons hot water, divided

¼–½ teaspoon matcha powder

¾ cup white grape juice

¾ cup white cranberry juice

5–6 freeze-dried strawberry slices

1. In a small bowl, combine strawberry powder and acai powder with 2–4 tablespoons hot water until a thick sauce consistency is reached. Stir and let bloom until you see tiny bubbles form on the surface (about 2 minutes). In a separate small bowl, combine matcha powder with 2–4 tablespoons hot water to form a bright green paste and let bloom (about 2 minutes).
2. Pour powder blends into a cocktail shaker filled with ice. Add grape juice and cranberry juice. Shake thoroughly.
3. Pour into a tall glass filled with ice and top with freeze-dried strawberry slices. Enjoy!

Coconut Morning Boost

Originally a drink to pick up in the drive-through, this recipe has been trending like crazy. The gatekeeping is over! People are talking about the Coconut Morning Boost because of its refreshing taste, antioxidants, and vibrant color. Its bright blue hue brings the whole airy vibe together—all natural, all clean, and heavenly good!

SERVES 1

2 tablespoons canned coconut cream, divided

1½ teaspoons blue spirulina powder, divided

½ medium banana, chopped and frozen

¼ medium avocado, peeled, pitted, chopped, and frozen

½ cup frozen pineapple chunks

¼ teaspoon collagen powder

½ teaspoon vanilla extract

1 tablespoon almond butter

1 tablespoon honey

1 cup almond milk

1. Place 1 tablespoon coconut cream into the bottom of a tall glass or 16-ounce clear plastic cup. Carefully add in ½ teaspoon blue spirulina powder, around the inside of the glass. (To help powder cling to the glass, you can dab some coconut cream around the inside of the glass first.) Set aside.
2. In a blender, add banana, avocado, pineapple, collagen powder, remaining 1 teaspoon blue spirulina powder, vanilla, almond butter, honey, and milk and blend until smooth and creamy.
3. Pour into the prepared glass and top with remaining 1 tablespoon coconut cream. If preferred, you can whip coconut cream before garnishing. Serve and enjoy!

Arnold Palmer

This perfect blend of iced tea meets lemonade has been popular for *decades*—and now you can make it at home! It's a simple recipe for bringing the summer barbecue vibes wherever you go. Keep the fun going with this classic creation.

SERVES 1

⅓ cup lemonade
⅔ cup iced tea
1 teaspoon lemon juice
2 lemon wheels

Fill a tall glass with ice and add lemonade, iced tea, and lemon juice. Stir well and garnish with lemon wheels.

Blueberry Tea Lemonade

Sometimes you just want a change of pace when it comes to tea flavors—and luckily, this Blueberry Tea Lemonade is the perfect match! The sweet, juicy taste of blueberry tea mixed with the tart punch of lemonade makes for a perfect spring or summertime drink (or, really, whenever you want it!).

SERVES 1

1 green tea bag
1 cup hot water
1 cup frozen blueberries
1 medium lemon, juiced, divided
2½ tablespoons honey, divided
4–6 fresh mint sprigs

1. In a mug, steep tea bag in water 5 minutes or until desired taste. Remove tea bag and refrigerate tea until cooled completely, 6 hours up to overnight.
2. In a small saucepan over medium-high heat, add blueberries, 1 tablespoon lemon juice, and 2 tablespoons honey. Cook 10–12 minutes until reduced to a syrup consistency.
3. Remove from heat and strain blueberries from syrup.
4. In a tall glass filled with ice, pour tea, remaining lemon juice, and remaining honey. Mix completely.
5. Carefully add blueberry syrup over ice and stir well. Garnish with mint sprigs.

#ForYou Tips

Like things a little more (or less) sweet? Just add more or less honey to the tea depending on what you prefer!

Brazilian Lemonade

Brazilian Lemonade takes very popular flavors—and the idea of a refreshing drink—to a whole new level. In Brazil, limes are more common than lemons, so despite the name, this is actually more like a limeade. It's got a sweet, slightly bitter flavoring, mixed with that green color everyone loves. You'll take one sip and never go back to plain lemonade 😋

SERVES 1

3 medium limes
¼ cup sweetened condensed milk
2 cups water
1 lime wheel

1. With a sharp knife, carefully remove just the green part of the lime peel and place in a blender. Juice limes and add to the blender. Add condensed milk and water and blend until smooth.
2. Pour into a tall glass and serve with a lime wheel for garnish.

#ForYou Tips

🔥 **If you're not a fan of pulp, you can strain the mixture before pouring it into glasses.**

Apple Crisp Refresher

The fall season is about more than pumpkins and hot lattes, and this drink proves it. This Apple Crisp Refresher encompasses the cozy fall flavors of apple, cinnamon, and ginger all in one sweet, refreshing cup.

SERVES 1

1 tablespoon caramel sauce
4 ounces ginger beer
4 ounces apple cider
3 ounces Sprite soda
1 teaspoon apple butter
½ ounce lemon juice
Ground cinnamon
1–2 apple slices

1. Pour caramel onto a clean plate. Carefully press the rim of a tall glass into caramel. Dip a frother in remaining caramel and carefully make circles on the inside of the glass.
2. Add ginger beer, apple cider, Sprite, apple butter, lemon juice, and some ice. Stir well.
3. Top with cinnamon and garnish with an apple slice or two. Enjoy!

#ForYou Tips

For a sharper flavor, add 2 more ounces each of ginger beer and apple cider.

Horchata

A Mexican favorite, horchata is more than just refreshing, it's creamy, cinnamony, and perfect for those days when you're on the go. This drink has been making its viral rounds, with so many people sharing their love and heritage via the recipe they've cherished for years. Each version may be a bit different, but each one, including this simple DIY, is beautifully refreshing!

SERVES 4

1½ cups long grain rice

4 cups water

2 cinnamon sticks

1 (12-ounce) can evaporated milk

½ (14-ounce) can sweetened condensed milk

2 teaspoons vanilla extract

1 teaspoon ground cinnamon

1. Rinse rice thoroughly and place in a small saucepan over high heat with water and cinnamon sticks. Heat until barely over a simmer. Turn off heat and let cool to room temperature. Refrigerate at least 24 hours.
2. In a large blender, add rice mixture and pulse 20 seconds.
3. Strain into a large bowl and remove chunks. Repeat this process, adding mixture back to blender, at least once more until all chunks are gone.
4. Pour mixture back in blender and add evaporated milk, condensed milk, vanilla, and ground cinnamon. Blend until combined and smooth. Pour into a pitcher and serve in tall glasses over some ice.

Taro Boba Tea

Boba is that perfect drink that combines creamy cold tea with sweet, chewy tapioca pearls. Perfect for any day of the year, this Taro Boba Tea isn't just iconic: It's the poster child for #kawaii. The taro flavoring is a sweet, nutty blend that pairs perfectly with the creamy vibes.

SERVES 2

1 cup tapioca pearls
3 tablespoons taro powder
1 cup brewed black tea, hot
¼ cup water
¼ cup packed dark brown sugar
3 cups whole milk

1. Boil tapioca pearls according to the package instructions, rinse with cold water, drain, and set aside.
2. Add taro powder to tea and mix well. Set aside to cool 5 minutes.
3. In a small saucepan over medium-high heat, combine water and sugar and stir until sugar dissolves. Reduce heat to low and simmer 8–10 minutes until thickened. Remove from heat and stir in tapioca pearls.
4. Assemble the drinks: Divide tapioca mixture between two glasses. Add tea and fill with ice. Pour milk on top and stir. Serve and enjoy!

#ForYou Tips

You can make other boba flavors like matcha or strawberry—just be sure to use the same amount of whatever powder flavor you choose.

Pineapple Iced Tea

Pineapple is *the* signature summer fruit—and what could taste more refreshing than that soothing flavor combined with refreshing iced tea?! Bursting with citrusy vibes, this easy recipe will be your new go-to for those #HotGirlSummer days 🔥

SERVES 4

4 cups water
4 green tea or lemon tea bags
1 cup pineapple juice
¼ cup lemon juice
3 tablespoons granulated sugar
4 pineapple wedges
4 lemon wheels

1. In a kettle, boil water. Add tea bags and steep 5–8 minutes (depending on desired taste). Remove tea bags and refrigerate kettle until cooled completely, 6 hours up to overnight.
2. In a pitcher filled with ice, add tea, pineapple juice, lemon juice, and sugar. Stir thoroughly. Pour into glasses and garnish with pineapple wedges and lemon wheels.

Sprite Iced Tea

Thanks to TikTok, people found out that tea mixed with Sprite can be the ultimate refreshing hack to quench your thirst. This Sprite Iced Tea is a delightful lemon twist in a bottle. All you need to do is place the tea bags in the soda bottle, turn it upside down, wait a bit, and you've got yourself a bubbly treat. It's two of the best viral drinks in one!

SERVES 4

5 lemon tea bags
1 (2-liter) bottle Sprite soda
2 medium lemons, halved

1. Place tea bags in Sprite bottle and close the bottle. Carefully turn upside down and let sit 1–2 hours until steeped.
2. Squeeze lemons evenly into four glasses filled halfway with ice. Then pour in Sprite mixture. Enjoy!

#ForYou Tips

Making it for one? Just use a smaller Sprite bottle and fewer tea bags. You can experiment with how many tea bags make for your preferred tea flavor.

CHAPTER 4

Sodas & Sparkling Beverages

Lemonade Blast with Raspberry Popping Boba

Add the delightful fun of popping boba to lemonade and you've got a blast of flavor delivered right to your taste buds! These little pearls pop with tart and sweet raspberry juice, turning every sip into a surprise. This TikTok drink doesn't just taste amazing, it's guaranteed to be your new go-to!

SERVES 2

1 cup raspberry juice

¼ tablespoon sodium alginate powder

2 tablespoons calcium lactate powder

4 cups warm water

3 cups lemonade

2 tablespoons blue curaçao syrup

1. In a blender, add raspberry juice and sodium alginate. Blend until completely smooth. Let sit 15–45 minutes until no air bubbles remain.
2. In a large bowl, mix calcium lactate with water until fully dissolved.
3. Using a dropper or small round spoon, gently drop sodium alginate mixture into calcium lactate bath. Let boba form 1–2 minutes, swirling occasionally so they don't stick together.
4. Scoop boba into a strainer and rinse twice in cold water.
5. Divide boba evenly across two tall glasses, then add lemonade. Fill glasses with ice and top with blue curaçao syrup.

Dirty Vanilla Coke

The classic Coke has gotten an upgrade! Thanks to Dirty Vanilla Coke recipes going around TikTok, you get to enjoy this treat at home. Delicious vanilla flavors swirling in bubbling Coke taste super luscious.

SERVES 1

1¼ cups Coke soda
½ tablespoon vanilla syrup
1 tablespoon vanilla-flavored coffee creamer

Fill a tall glass with ice. Pour in Coke and vanilla syrup. Top with creamer. Mix and enjoy!

Baja Twist

The Baja Blast is all over the place—so much bigger than trendiness itself, that iconic green color is a whole vibe on its own! This twist on the fan fave is made for anyone who loves amped-up lemon-lime sips.

SERVES 1

⅓ cup Sprite soda
⅓ cup Mountain Dew soda
⅓ cup blue Powerade

Fill a large glass halfway with ice, then pour in Sprite, Mountain Dew, and Powerade. Stir and enjoy!

Dr Pepper Cherry Dirty Soda

This dirty soda mixes some of the most viral flavors into one. Dr Pepper Cherry has been having a ✨ moment, ✨ and people can't deny the goodness. And making it creamy just takes it to a whole new level. It's like a better version of a Dr Pepper float!

SERVES 1

1 tablespoon cherry syrup
1 cup Dr Pepper Cherry soda
1 tablespoon original-flavored creamer

In a 12-ounce cup, add cherry syrup and Dr Pepper and mix. Top with creamer.

Strawberry Popping Boba Float

Popping boba are irresistible and satisfying, giving an exploding burst of flavor in every sip. Combined with ice cream and creamy sparkling soda, this Strawberry Popping Boba Float is a melt-in-your-mouth experience 🤤

SERVES 1

½ cup strawberry ice cream
1 (12-ounce) can vanilla-flavored soda
¼ cup strawberry popping boba

In a tall glass, add ice cream and pour in soda. Place popping boba gently over top. Stir and enjoy!

Italian Soda

A subtly sweet drink made right, this version of viral Italian Soda is the bright, delectable drink of the season. It's the easiest (and yummiest) way to feel refreshed within seconds!

SERVES 1

1 ounce vanilla syrup
1 ounce raspberry syrup
2 ounces cherry syrup
12 ounces club soda
2–3 maraschino cherries

In a tall glass filled with ice, add in your syrups and top with club soda. Mix it all up and garnish with maraschino cherries.

Fluffy Soda

Fluffy Soda has been having its moment online because of how alluring the concept is. To get that fluffy coating, it requires a brush of Marshmallow Fluff around the inside of a glass and then a downstream of delicious soda flavor. *Sooo* refreshing!

SERVES 1

2 tablespoons Marshmallow Fluff

1 (12-ounce) can cola soda

1. Spread Fluff along the inside of a tall glass, making swirls and patterns.
2. Fill glass with soda to the rim. Stir and enjoy!

#ForYou Tips

To fit different themes, you can add certain shapes with the Marshmallow Fluff, like little ghosts for spooky season. Make faces on the outside of the glass or cup for the ghosts or other creatures!

Dirty Shirley Temple

Dirty sodas go beyond just the traditional Coke and creamer. You can make them with fruity drinks too, and the taste is just as impressive. This sweet, satisfying Dirty Shirley Temple will definitely make your taste buds go wild. Its mellow cherry flavoring combined with a creamy texture makes for something you'll wanna keep drinking. And luckily, it's easy to make it for any mood!

SERVES 1

1 cup lemon-lime soda
1 tablespoon grenadine
2 tablespoons vanilla creamer
3 maraschino cherries

1. In a tall glass filled halfway with ice, add soda and grenadine. Stir until combined.
2. Lightly pour in creamer and top with maraschino cherries.

Spicy Watermelon Soda

Watermelon is one of those classics where it's perfect anytime (and anyplace) you want a refreshing and sweet taste. And this spicy soda is a perfect way to incorporate that watermelon flavor into something with a kick. A salty rim, sweet juice, bubbly soda, and spicy chamoy and Tajín—what could be more perfect for summer vibes?!

SERVES 2

1 tablespoon chamoy sauce

3 tablespoons Tajín seasoning, plus more for garnish

1 cup cubed watermelon

Juice from ½ medium lime

1 (12-ounce) can lemon-lime soda

½ medium jalapeño pepper, sliced

1. Rim two glasses with chamoy and dip in a plate of Tajín. Set aside.
2. Place watermelon in a blender and blend until smooth. Strain out pulp and divide juice into two glasses.
3. Add lime juice into the glasses, and soda over top.
4. Top with jalapeños and a little more Tajín. Enjoy!

Cherry Lime Float

Calling all cherry lovers, this drink is for you! The viral Cherry Lime Float is a level up to any OG and for good reason! It doesn't just look pretty but tastes absolutely delectable. With a smooth, creamy blend mixed with a sweet, tart cherry flavor, this drink will satisfy any craving you're having any time of day.

SERVES 1

2 tablespoons lime juice
¼ cup maraschino cherry syrup
½ cup Sprite soda
1 cup vanilla ice cream
2 maraschino cherries
1 lime wheel

1. In a tall glass, combine lime juice and maraschino cherry syrup. Mix well.
2. Pour Sprite into the glass and top with ice cream. Garnish with maraschino cherries and lime wheel. Slowly stir and enjoy!

Jelly Soda

Aesthetic drinks are all the hype, and this Jelly Soda looks just as good as it tastes. Think pink, purple, and more pink!

SERVES 2

½ cup cold water
2 (0.25-ounce) packets unflavored gelatin
1 cup purple Powerade
1 cup pink lemonade
2 (12-ounce) cans cherry vanilla soda

1. Lightly grease two (5½") square baking dishes.
2. Pour ¼ cup cold water into each of two small glasses. Sprinkle 1 packet gelatin in each glass. Stir to mix, then set aside 5 minutes to bloom until gelatin has absorbed all water.
3. In a small saucepan over medium-high heat, add Powerade and heat to a simmer, then remove from heat. Add one bloomed gelatin mixture and stir until dissolved. Slowly pour into one of the prepared dishes and try to avoid creating bubbles. Refrigerate until set, at least 6 hours.
4. Repeat step 3 with pink lemonade and second gelatin mixture.
5. Carefully remove set gelatin from baking dishes and cut into ½" or smaller cubes.
6. Divide purple and pink jelly cubes into two tall glasses. Fill glasses halfway with ice and add soda. Stir and enjoy!

#ForYou Tips

For extra flavor, you can swap the unflavored gelatin for 1 (3-ounce) flavored gelatin packet.

Jolly Rancher Soda

Jolly Ranchers are *huge* online, so why not make them a little more interesting by giving them their own soda?! This drink is bursting with nostalgic candy flavor in every sip—so satisfying and delicious!

SERVES 2

3 cups lemon-lime soda, divided

10–14 same-flavored Jolly Rancher candies of choice

1. In a small saucepan over high heat, heat 1 cup soda with Jolly Ranchers until candies are fully melted, about 10 minutes. Let cool completely, about 1 hour.
2. Divide Jolly Rancher liquid into two glasses filled halfway with ice. Pour remaining soda over top. Enjoy!

Sour Patch Fizz

Nothing tastes better than the classic twist of candy in a drink, and this Sour Patch Fizz is unmatched for delight. This drink is so delicious and made for those times where you just wanna feel like a kid again!

SERVES 2

1 (8-ounce) bag Sour Patch Kids candy

1 (12-ounce) can lemon-lime soda

4 ounces Ghost Energy drink

1 tablespoon blue raspberry syrup

1. Place 2–3 Sour Patch Kids of assorted colors in each section of an ice tray. Fill tray with water and freeze until solid.
2. Fill two glasses with candy ice cubes. In each glass, pour 6 ounces soda, 2 ounces energy drink, and 1½ teaspoons blue raspberry syrup.
3. Top off with more Sour Patch Kids and enjoy!

#ForYou Tips

If you don't like energy drinks, you can swap them out for equal parts Capri-Sun!

Triple Berry Sparkler

When it comes to sparklers, the most important thing to get straight is not skimping on the ice cubes. That's why this Triple Berry Sparkler went viral, because not only are you getting some refreshing bubbles out of it, but when the ice melts, it changes the flavor from sweet to tart, making every sip perfection. It will be your new poolside obsession 🥰

SERVES 2

⅓ cup fresh raspberries
⅓ cup chopped fresh strawberries
⅓ cup fresh blueberries
1⅓ cups coconut water
2 tablespoons honey
2 tablespoons lemon juice
2 tablespoons lime juice
1⅓ cups soda water or seltzer

1. Places berries in a standard-sized ice tray, mixing and matching for multiple flavors. Fill tray with coconut water and freeze until solid.
2. In a small pitcher, gently mix honey, lemon juice, lime juice, and soda water.
3. Fill two glasses with berry ice cubes and top with soda mixture. Stir each drink and enjoy!

Strawberry Lemon Spritz

You've probably seen people making sparkling lemonade, but this Strawberry Lemon Spritz is an upgrade you'll wanna enjoy for yourself. It blends the crisp, refreshing flavors of sweet and sour all in one cup! Perfect for any time of year, this bubbly sipper is a tasty way to cap off your night or get you through long work hours.

SERVES 2

3 fresh strawberries, diced
2 lemon wedges
2 cups lemonade
2 cups sparkling water
2 fresh strawberries, sliced
2 lemon wheels

1. In a glass, muddle strawberries and lemon wedges until mixture is mostly juice. Remove lemon wedges and strain mixture into two glasses.
2. Add ice to fill. Pour 1 cup lemonade and 1 cup sparkling water into each glass.
3. Garnish each glass with a strawberry slice and a lemon wheel.

Sparkling Shaved Fruit

Shaved fruit has been all the rage on social media. The simple trick of grating your favorite frozen fruits and enjoying it like a sorbet is *genius*. And this drink is the best of both worlds, combining the refreshing taste of the viral trend with sparkling water!

SERVES 2

½ medium peach, frozen
6 whole strawberries, frozen
½ medium mango, frozen
1 (12-ounce) can flavored sparkling drink

1. In separate small bowls, grate each frozen fruit. Layer the different flavors together in two tall glasses.
2. Slowly pour sparkling drink over top. This drink works with both a spoon and a straw!

#ForYou Tips

You can use a grating machine or shaved ice machine to make things a little easier (and keep your fingers from getting cold!).

Glitter (Rainbow) Drink

This Glitter (Rainbow) Drink brings the celestial vibes to your glass, with beautiful edible glitter swirling like stars. This drink went megaviral for good reason. Stir the layers all together and you get a delicious, soft bubbly with some energizing, refreshing taste!

SERVES 1

⅛ teaspoon butterfly pea flower powder

¼ cup water

2 tablespoons grenadine

¼ teaspoon silver edible glitter

½ cup tropical Red Bull

½ cup blue Powerade

1. In a small measuring cup, combine butterfly pea flower and water. Set aside.
2. Pour grenadine into a tall glass and add some ice. Carefully pour glitter over the ice.
3. Slowly pour in Red Bull, then Powerade to form a layer on top. Add a final layer of butterfly pea flower mixture. Serve and enjoy!

#ForYou Tips

To help make the layers distinct, use a bar spoon and gently pour each layer over the back of the spoon so they form evenly.

CHAPTER 5

Frozen & Dessert Drinks

Affogato

Italy sure stepped up its game when it came up with the affogato, and now trending practically across the world, people are absolutely *loving it*! This creamy coffee drink is so delectable, it's kind of like an iced cappuccino in a cup. It can be eaten with a spoon or you can let the ice cream melt and sip it.

SERVES 1

1 cup vanilla ice cream
1 ounce freshly brewed espresso
1 teaspoon grated dark chocolate

1. Place ice cream in a small mug or glass. Pour espresso over ice cream. Sprinkle grated chocolate on top.
2. Stir and enjoy sipping, or watch the espresso drizzle and eat with a spoon.

Pineapple Whip Float

Pineapples trend harder than life itself, and when paired with vanilla ice cream, nothing screams summer like the Pineapple Whip Float This drink tastes even better than it looks! Wanna avoid dairy? Just use coconut milk! Add a 13.5-ounce can, along with ½ cup granulated sugar and ice to fill, in place of the ice cream.

SERVES 1

2 cups frozen pineapple chunks
½ cup pineapple juice
1 cup vanilla ice cream
1 pineapple wedge

1. In a blender, add pineapple chunks and pineapple juice and blend until smooth. Add ice cream and pulse until combined.
2. Pour into a tall glass and garnish with a pineapple wedge.

#ForYou Tips

If you want this to be an even thicker consistency, put the blended mixture in a bag fitted with a piping tip and freeze it 2–4 hours before piping it into the glass and topping with a pineapple wedge.

Cracked Dubai Chocolate Milkshake

Dubai chocolate is already a showstopper, and people are making it into absolutely everything! So what happens when you mix it with the Internet's favorite cracked trend? The *ultimate* Cracked Dubai Chocolate Milkshake: a rich and decadent delight that cracks with every sip.

SERVES 2

2 (4-ounce) bars semisweet baking chocolate, chopped

1 tablespoon unsalted butter

1 cup kataifi

1 (150-gram) jar pistachio cream

4 cups vanilla ice cream

Canned whipped cream

2 tablespoons pistachios, chopped

1. Over medium-low heat, place chocolate in the top of a double boiler or a heatproof bowl set over a pan of simmering water. Stir constantly until melted, about 10 minutes, being careful not to let the temperature exceed 90°F. Pour melted chocolate into a 16-ounce clear, flexible plastic cup and coat the inside by swirling chocolate around the cup. Pour remaining chocolate back into the bowl. Repeat with a second cup. Freeze 3 minutes, until hardened.
2. Melt butter in a large skillet over medium heat. Add kataifi and cook 2–3 minutes, stirring, until golden. Stir in pistachio cream. Transfer to a paper towel–lined plate and set aside 5 minutes.
3. Add ice cream and kataifi-pistachio mixture to a blender. Pulse gently 2–4 times until just combined but still thick and textured.
4. Pour into chocolate-coated cups, then top with whipped cream and chopped pistachios. Crack, sip, and enjoy!

Frozen Hot Chocolate

Hot chocolate is getting a temperature downgrade—and in this case, that's a good thing. Thanks to the Frozen Hot Chocolate hype, you can enjoy the OG chocolatey flavors year-round in a creamy, cold smoothie!

SERVES 2

3 cups ice

2 cups chocolate milk

2 (1.3-ounce) packets powdered hot chocolate mix

Canned whipped cream

2 teaspoons semisweet baking chocolate shavings

1. In a large blender, add ice, milk, and hot chocolate mix. Blend until completely smooth.
2. Pour mixture into two tall glasses and top with whipped cream and chocolate shavings.

Cookie Monster Milkshake

Sometimes you just wanna sink into some childhood nostalgia—and the Cookie Monster Milkshake does just that (with a little extra)! With a light cocoa taste and creamy vanilla twist, this drink didn't get its name in the spotlight just on vibes alone. It's a superindulgent treat where every bite is full of cookie goodness.

SERVES 2

8 Chips Ahoy! cookies, divided
10 Oreo cookies, divided
4 tablespoons vanilla frosting
1 pint vanilla ice cream
¼ cup whole milk
4–5 drops blue food coloring
Canned whipped cream

1. On a small plate, crumble 2 Chips Ahoy! cookies and 2 Oreo cookies.
2. Spread frosting around the top of two glasses or mugs, making a 1"–2" rim. Roll the rims in cookie crumbs and press to adhere.
3. In a large blender, add ice cream, milk, and food coloring and blend until smooth. Add 6 Oreo cookies and 4 Chips Ahoy! cookies. Blend thoroughly. If mixture seems too thick, add more milk to thin it out.
4. Pour milkshake into the prepared glasses. Garnish each with whipped cream, 1 Oreo cookie, and 1 Chips Ahoy! cookie.

Unicorn Frappuccino Redux

Every few years, a fancy unicorn drink goes viral, but through all the different types, and sour/tart flavors, there are usually mixed reviews. Luckily, the Starbucks Unicorn Frappuccino has been all the rave since it came out—and this twist on the brand fave is so full of fruity, luscious flavors you'll wanna post about it yourself!

SERVES 2

¼ cup white chocolate chips

2 tablespoons sweetened condensed milk

2 tablespoons heavy whipping cream

2–3 drops blue food coloring

2 teaspoons blue raspberry lemonade Kool-Aid drink mix

1 cup ice

1 cup frozen mango chunks

3–4 drops pink food coloring

2 cups vanilla ice cream

½ cup whole milk

Canned whipped cream

Pink and blue decorating sugar

1. In a small bowl, microwave chocolate in 15-second intervals until mostly melted. Stir in condensed milk and cream. Add blue food coloring and Kool-Aid. Pour into a squeeze bottle.
2. In a blender, add ice, mango, and pink food coloring and blend until smooth. Add ice cream and whole milk and pulse until just combined.
3. Drizzle the inside of two tall glasses or plastic cups with blue chocolate drizzle. Slowly pour ice cream mixture into the glasses. Top each with whipped cream. Sprinkle with pink and blue sugar.

#ForYou Tips

Swap out the mango and food coloring for frozen dragon fruit for a natural pink color!

Frozen Whipped Lemonade

TikTok wasn't playing around when this drink hit the viral spotlight. Frozen Whipped Lemonade is a creamy mix of sweet, sour, and blended refreshingness. The best thing is that it's made in minutes, perfect for those hot summer days when you don't have time to sit (IOW, sweat) around waiting on a cold drink 🥰

SERVES 2

1–2 medium lemons, zested and juiced
½ cup heavy cream
¼ cup sweetened condensed milk
2 cups ice
Canned whipped cream

1. In a blender, add ¼ cup lemon juice, cream, condensed milk, and ice and blend until smooth.
2. Pour into two cups, top with whipped cream, sprinkle lemon zest over top, and enjoy!

Frosted Soda

Frosted Soda is the Internet's dream of soft ice cream meets soda. Originally created by the favorite drive-through chicken spot, it takes the root beer float and gives it a full makeover, with an irresistible texture and sweet, swirled flavors. This version is a tasty adventure of soda and creamy ice cream all wrapped up in one—where you get to choose any flavor twists you want!

SERVES 2

1 (12-ounce) can soda of choice
1½ cups vanilla ice cream
Canned whipped cream (optional)

1. In a blender, pour soda and ice cream. Pulse and then blend until creamy and smooth.
2. Serve in two glasses, topped with whipped cream if preferred.

#ForYou Tips

You can mix and match different flavors of soda together! Try cream soda, root beer, Dr Pepper, or orange soda.

Firecracker Frozen Slushie

Things are super festive thanks to this Firecracker Frozen Slushie, which layers red, white, and blue colors. This icy cold drink is perfect for those barbecues and hot summer days (or anytime you want it!).

SERVES 2

For Blue Layer

¼ cup blue curaçao

1½ cups ice

1 cup lemonade

For White Layer

1½ cups ice

1 cup lemonade

For Red Layer

¼ cup maraschino cherry syrup

¼ cup lemonade

1½ cups ice

2 Bomb Pop ice pops, for garnish

1. Make Blue Layer: In a blender, add blue layer ingredients and blend until smooth, then pour into two tall glasses.
2. Make White Layer: Clean blender. Add white layer ingredients and blend until smooth. Pour over blue layer in each glass.
3. Make Red Layer: Blend red layer ingredients until smooth and pour mixture over white layer in each glass.
4. Garnish each drink with a Bomb Pop and serve immediately.

#ForYou Tips

In between making each layer, place the glasses in the freezer to keep each prior layer nice and firm.

Viral Frozen Gummy Bears

Gummy bears are making a huge comeback, thanks to this frozen gummy bear hack! In this recipe, the nostalgic candies go from chewy to icy overnight. With each bite tasting so satisfyingly sweet, you can bite right through them like butter. It's like a slushie you get to eat.

SERVES 2

1 cup gummy bears

2½ cups Sprite soda

1. Place gummy bears in a single layer in a container with a lid. Pour in enough Sprite to cover gummy bears completely. Cover and refrigerate 24 hours.
2. Remove from refrigerator and open container. Gummy bears should have doubled in size. Drain liquid and place gummies on a small baking sheet lined with parchment paper. Freeze 3 hours. Enjoy!

#ForYou Tips

Try out other types of soda for different flavors!

Thin Mint Frosted Shake

There's no denying that these mint cookies are addictive, so of course when the Thin Mints Frosty went viral, it was for good reason! This deliciously thick take on the fan fave is both scoopable *and* drinkable. Plus, it's perfectly minty and chocolatey in flavor.

SERVES 2

For Chocolate Ganache

½ cup heavy cream
½ cup semisweet chocolate chips
¼ teaspoon mint extract

For Shakes

4 cups vanilla ice cream
6 Thin Mints cookies
½ teaspoon mint extract
¼ cup whole milk
1 cup Cool Whip topping
Canned whipped cream
6 Thin Mints cookies, crushed

1. To Make Chocolate Ganache: In a small saucepan over low, heat heavy cream to a simmer (barely boil). Remove from heat and add in chocolate chips and mint extract. Slowly stir until mixture is combined and drizzle falls. Set aside.
2. To Make Shakes: In a blender, add ice cream, Thin Mints, mint extract, milk, and Cool Whip. Blend until smooth.
3. Drizzle 2–3 tablespoons Chocolate Ganache into two tall glasses and pour in Shakes. Drizzle more Chocolate Ganache over top and top with whipped cream and crushed Thin Mints. Serve and enjoy!

Soft Ice Slushie

Soft ice is one of the coolest drinks that ever hit #DrinkTok. And we're lucky it did! Solid and liquid at the exact same time, this drink makes an icy effect when it's poured. It's nature's most engaging science experiment!

SERVES 1

1 (16.9-ounce) plastic bottle purified water, unopened

1. Freeze water bottle 2 hours exactly. It should still be in a liquid state after 2 hours.
2. Remove from freezer, slam bottom of bottle on a hard surface, and watch it start to crystallize.
3. Over a cold plate, pour water into a tower. It should start to get taller and freeze as you pour. Enjoy with a spoon or straw!

Almost a Shamrock Shake

The Shamrock Shake has us all in a choke hold, especially during the green festivities of Saint Patrick's Day. And now you get to re-create the same great minty flavors and vibrant color at home any time of year—no drive-through required. This version might not be served in a plastic cup with golden arches, but it's just as good as the OG.

SERVES 2

1 pint vanilla ice cream
½ cup whole milk
¼ teaspoon mint extract
3–4 drops green food coloring
Canned whipped cream

1. In a large blender, add ice cream, milk, mint, and food coloring and blend until smooth.
2. Pour into two Mason jar mugs, top with whipped cream, and enjoy!

Kinder Bueno Milkshake

There's something so gratifying about making a drink that requires little to no effort, and this Kinder Bueno Milkshake hits the mark on that. Made to match the creamy, chocolatey flavors of the popular Kinder Bueno chocolate bar, you'll be begging for more than just one glass. Good thing this recipe makes enough for two! 😋

SERVES 2

¼ cup plus 1 tablespoon chocolate syrup, divided

1 pint vanilla ice cream

¼–½ cup whole milk

4 (0.75-ounce) Kinder Bueno chocolate bars, divided

Canned whipped cream

1. Pour ¼ cup chocolate syrup around the inside of two tall glasses or mugs and set aside.
2. In a large blender, add ice cream, ¼ cup milk, and 2 chocolate bars and blend until smooth. If you prefer a thinner texture, add another ¼ cup milk and blend.
3. Pour into prepared glasses. Top with whipped cream and drizzle remaining 1 tablespoon chocolate syrup over top. Garnish with remaining chocolate bars. Enjoy!

Watermelon Lime Slushie

There's nothing that says summer as much as the sweet, tart flavors of a viral Watermelon Lime Slushie. This icy treat is delicious *and* quenching for those superhot days.

SERVES 2

2 cups ice
1½ cups cubed watermelon
1 medium lime, zested and juiced
5–6 fresh mint leaves
2 lime wheels

1. In a large blender, add ice, watermelon, lime juice, and lime zest, saving some zest for garnish. Blend until smooth.
2. Pour into two glasses. Add remaining zest to garnish, along with mint and lime wheels.

Peanut Butter Cup Oreo Milkshake

What's even better than an Oreo milkshake? A Peanut Butter Cup Oreo Milkshake! Combining two of the most popular flavors into one, this milkshake is definitely worth the hype. This recipe is the perfect size for sharing with your fave, or you can up the indulgence and enjoy it all for yourself.

SERVES 2

8 Oreo cookies, divided
10 miniature Reese's peanut butter cups, divided
¼ cup whole milk
3 cups vanilla ice cream
Canned whipped cream

1. In a blender, add 6 Oreos, 8 peanut butter cups, and milk. Blend until smooth.
2. Add ice cream and slowly pulse until combined, adding more milk if needed.
3. Pour into two glasses and top with whipped cream and 1 Oreo per glass. Crumble remaining peanut butter cups and sprinkle on top. Enjoy!

Almost a Grimace Shake

The Grimace Shake is more than just an homage to the nostalgic monster that fast-food fans know and love; it's an indie horror scene splattered *purple*. Yup, the drink from the classic restaurant chain brought people together through an unexpected viral TikTok trend where people would "go AWOL" once they drank it. But despite the freaky trend to "drop dead" once ingested, this purple berry milkshake is absolutely delicious and deserves all the hype. This take on the popular offering just has one warning of its own: You'll be coming back for more, and more, and more!

SERVES 2

1 cup frozen blueberries
½ cup frozen strawberries
½ cup frozen raspberries
¼ cup whole milk
3 cups vanilla ice cream
Canned whipped cream (optional)

1. In a blender, add berries and milk and blend until fully smooth. If needed, add more milk and blend again.
2. Add ice cream and slowly pulse until mixture is fully combined. Pour into two tall glasses and top with whipped cream if desired.

CHAPTER 6

Entertaining

Butterfly Pea Flower Tea Lemonade

Nothing beats a party with a cool color-changing drink, and this one hits that mark on *sooo* many levels. The Butterfly Pea Flower Tea Lemonade has gone viral due to its ability to change from blue to pink, creating a vibrant, beautiful concoction perfect for a gathering with friends. So sit back and relax with your besties—you've got yourself an entertainment piece *and* a tasty delight 🤤

SERVES 6

1 cup water
2 tablespoons granulated sugar
1 teaspoon butterfly pea flower powder
6 cups lemonade
6 lemon wedges

1. In a small saucepan over medium heat, combine water, sugar, and butterfly pea flower powder. Heat and stir until warm and about to bubble, 5–6 minutes. Remove from heat and cool completely, about 30 minutes.
2. Fill six tall glasses with ice and pour 1 cup lemonade into each glass. Slowly pour 2 tablespoons brewed butterfly pea flower tea over the back of a spoon into each glass so it lies above the lemonade.
3. Garnish each glass with a lemon wedge and serve.

#ForYou Tips

Wanna make this easy for guests to serve themselves? Add the butterfly pea flower tea to a jug and pour the lemonade over top or have each person add lemonade to their own glass of tea. 😋

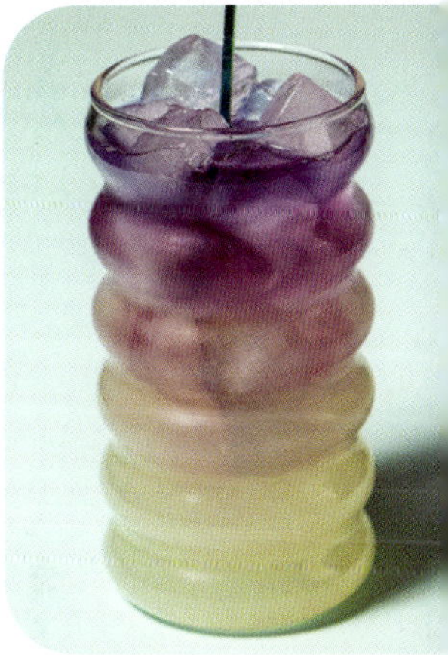

Snow Globe Drink

If there's one thing the holidays are for, it's coming together to share in festive food—and drinks! Unmatched for its cute party trick, this viral Snow Globe Drink will have your guests talking. Perfect with absolutely any spritzer or refreshing clear drink on top, it tastes just like that holiday magic we all get excited about! While the recipe calls for 6 cranberries per glass, feel free to get super festive and use as many cranberries as you like for your snow globes!

SERVES 6

Clear soda, divided
6 sprigs fresh rosemary
36 fresh cranberries

1. Fill six short glasses ⅓ way with soda. Carefully place 6 cranberries and 1 upside-down rosemary sprig in each glass. Place glasses in freezer, making sure rosemary sprigs are standing upright. Freeze overnight until completely solid, at least 8 hours.
2. Remove glasses from freezer and top off with remaining soda. Serve!

#ForYou Tips

You can use string to help prop up the rosemary sprig before freezing so it doesn't get lopsided.

Adult Capri-Sun

The Adult Capri-Sun has gone viral for its nostalgic taste of childhood—with a grown-up twist. This large-batch recipe is perfect for sharing at any adults-only gathering.

SERVES 6

6 (6-ounce) pouches Capri-Sun, flavor of choice

6 ounces vodka

1 (16-ounce) bag frozen mixed fruit

1. Carefully cut open Capri-Sun pouches as close to the top as possible. Pour out a little liquid from each pouch.
2. Top each Capri-Sun with 1 ounce vodka and 2–4 frozen fruits. Place a straw in each pouch and enjoy!

Mermaid Water Cocktail

Say goodbye to cucumber spa water because the Mermaid Water Cocktail is taking those relaxing vibes to another level. This easy mix of coconut, pineapple, and lime will get people ready to party until the sun sets!

SERVES 6

18–24 lime wheels

12 ounces spiced rum

6 ounces coconut rum

18 ounces pineapple juice

6 ounces blue curaçao

3 ounces lime juice

1. In six tall glasses with a little ice, carefully arrange 3–4 lime wheels in each glass, with one sitting on the rim.
2. In a large pitcher, add all remaining ingredients and stir thoroughly. Pour into prepared glasses.

Electric Lemonade

This alcoholic drink tastes like a sour gummy—sweet and tart all in one cup. But the true aesthetic comes with its bright, bold blue color. It will make any gathering a ten out of ten in seconds.

SERVES 6

6 ounces lemon-flavored vodka
6 ounces blue curaçao
18 ounces sour mix
24 ounces Sprite soda

1. In a large cocktail shaker filled with ice, add vodka, blue curaçao, and sour mix. Shake 2–3 minutes until chilled. You may need to work in batches.
2. Pour mixture into six tall glasses. Top each with Sprite and serve.

Peach Sangria

This tasty twist on classic white wine sangria is bright and fresh and will make the next hang truly something to remember.

SERVES 6–8

3 medium peaches, pitted and sliced
6–7 fresh strawberries, sliced
12 fresh raspberries
1 (750 mL) bottle dry white wine
¼ cup peach schnapps
2 tablespoons lemon juice
½ cup club soda

1. In a large pitcher, mix fruit, wine, peach schnapps, and lemon juice. Refrigerate until ready to serve, up to overnight.
2. When ready to serve, add in some ice and club soda. Pour into glasses and enjoy!

Blackberry Spritz in a Jam Jar

This blackberry spritz will impress your guests and get them talking. The best part? It's made in a jam jar! This refreshing cocktail is a breath of fresh air, highlighting the sweet and tart flavors of the summer. Plus how cute is it to serve drinks in tiny jars?!

SERVES 4

14 fresh blackberries, divided
8 large fresh mint leaves
1 tablespoon lemon juice
¼ cup simple syrup
½ cup prosecco
½ cup Vizzy Hard Seltzer or sparkling water
4 small sprigs fresh mint

1. In a small bowl, muddle 6 blackberries, mint leaves, lemon juice, and simple syrup until mixture forms a smooth paste.
2. Add about 1 tablespoon blackberry mixture into each of the 4 (8-ounce) jam jars.
3. Divide prosecco and seltzer among the jars. Top each jar with remaining blackberries and mint sprigs. Enjoy!

Bonne Maman
Raspberry
LAMARCA
PROSECCO

Cherry Lemon Jell-O Shots

No party is complete without Jell-O shots 🔥 This sweet, tart recipe went viral right in its summer prime! It offers the perfect aesthetic for all the best gatherings.

SERVES 12

6 medium lemons

1½ cups water, divided

2 (0.25-ounce) packets unflavored gelatin

1 (3-ounce) packet cherry-flavored gelatin mix

1 cup vodka

1. Cut each lemon in half vertically. To create bowls with lemon halves, scoop out insides and place into a juicer. Squeeze juice into a bowl fitted with a strainer. Discard excess pulp and set aside lemon rinds.
2. Add ½ cup water and unflavored gelatin to juice. Whisk and set aside 5 minutes, until gelatin has absorbed all liquid.
3. Place cherry gelatin mix in a medium bowl and add 1 cup boiling water. Whisk until powder dissolves. Add lemon gelatin mixture and whisk until smooth. Allow to cool to room temperature, about 10 minutes. Stir in vodka.
4. Carefully pour mixture into lemon rinds. Fill each to the top and pop any bubbles with a spoon. Refrigerate uncovered overnight until set.
5. Rinse a sharp knife with warm water and cut each lemon half into three wedges. Refrigerate until ready to serve.

#ForYou Tips

To keep the filled lemons steady, place each half in the cup of a muffin pan.

Hawaiian Mimosa

What's better than a classic mimosa over breakfast with friends? This viral Hawaiian twist! The beloved mimosa flavors are now infused with coconut and pineapple for a perfect addition to those summer bashes, bestie brunches, or pool parties!

SERVES 6

15 ounces pineapple juice
6 ounces coconut rum
24 ounces sparkling wine
3 ounces grenadine
6 small pineapple wedges
6 maraschino cherries

1. Pour 2½ ounces pineapple juice and 1 ounce rum in each of the six champagne flutes. Top each glass with 4 ounces sparkling wine.
2. Slowly pour ½ ounce grenadine over the back of a spoon into each glass, allowing grenadine to sink to the bottom and create a nice gradient.
3. For each garnish, place 1 pineapple wedge and 1 maraschino cherry on rim of each glass and serve.

Dragon Fruit Hwachae

This Dragon Fruit Hwachae took the lead on #DrinkTok because of its refreshing taste. Those 3 a.m. cravings are no longer now that you have a bowl of fresh fruit *and* an aesthetic drink all in one. Made with trendy dragon fruit, it's one of the best homemade refreshers!

SERVES 4–6

2 cups cubed watermelon
½ cup fresh raspberries
¼ cup diced fresh strawberries
1 medium pink dragon fruit, cubed
1 medium white dragon fruit, cubed
2 cups coconut jellies
1¾ cups Almost a Pink Drink (see recipe in Chapter 3)
2⅛ cups Sprite soda
4 cups ice

In a large serving bowl, add watermelon, raspberries, strawberries, pink and white dragon fruit, coconut jellies, Almost a Pink Drink, and Sprite. Carefully add in ice and mix. Ladle into individual glasses or bowls for serving.

#ForYou Tips

Do not use milk or any products containing dairy or else the drink will curdle!

Sparkling Punch

The classic of any hit gathering is a big bowl of punch, but what makes it better? When anyone, including the kids, can get in on the goodness! This nonalcoholic Sparkling Punch is bursting with citrusy, sweet flavors and bubbles perfect for any occasion.

SERVES 6

¼ cup orange juice
2 tablespoons strawberry Kool-Aid drink mix
4 (12-ounce) cans lemon-lime soda
2 (12-ounce) cans orange soda
2 medium oranges, sliced
½ cup sliced fresh strawberries
2 medium lemons, sliced

1. In a large punch bowl, mix orange juice, Kool-Aid, and sodas.
2. Carefully add sliced fruit on top. Serve alongside cups.

Caramel Apple Cider

Move over, pumpkin spice, apples are having a ✨ moment ✨ And looking at this Caramel Apple Cider, there's no doubt why! This spiced, crispy sensation will keep you warm through those cozy falls and winters. It's the perfect mug pleaser when things get chilly.

SERVES 6

6 cups apple cider

4 teaspoons ground cinnamon

2 cinnamon sticks

2 medium honeycrisp apples, sliced

¼ cup caramel sauce, plus more for garnish

Canned whipped cream

1. In a medium pot, mix apple cider, ground cinnamon, cinnamon sticks, and apples. Bring to boil over high heat, then reduce heat to low and simmer 10 minutes.
2. Spread caramel along the inside of six heatproof glasses or mugs. Pour cider mix in each glass. Top with whipped cream and drizzle more caramel over top. Enjoy!

Witches' Brew

Watch out because this Witches' Brew will have your guests shaking in terror! Frothy, bubbly, green, and eerily tempting, this cauldron is a sweet tooth's dream. Go wild and use as many of gooey worms, eyeball candies, sprinkles, and lime wedges as you like. You can also add a spooky smoke effect by topping each glass with dry ice—just be sure to follow safe handling instructions!

SERVES 10

1½ cups lime sorbet
2 cups lemonade
1 cup Sprite soda
1 cup green Hawaiian Punch (or pineapple juice)
½ cup ginger ale
3 drops green food coloring
Gummy worms
Gummy eyeball candies
Halloween-themed sprinkles
Lime wedges

Add all ingredients to a large punch bowl. Mix together and ladle into small cups or glasses to serve. Enjoy!

Mango Sago

When it comes to the Internet, it's always mango season, and Mango Sago is no exception! With its irresistible creamy texture, each bite is different—and *sooo* ridiculously good. This has *got* to be your new showstopper for a crowd: Everyone will be raving about it afterward.

SERVES 4

1 (3-ounce) packet orange-flavored gelatin mix

1 cup sago pearls

2 medium ripe mangos, peeled, pitted, and sliced

¼ cup water

¼ cup sweetened condensed milk

¾ cup evaporated milk

3 large ripe mangos, peeled, pitted, and cut into chunks

1. Make gelatin mix according to package instructions, omitting cold water. Pour into an ice tray that makes small shapes and refrigerate 2–4 hours until completely firm.
2. In a medium saucepan over high heat, cook sago pearls according to package instructions until they turn translucent. Strain and rinse with cold water. Set aside.
3. Place mango slices in a blender with water and blend until a thick smoothie consistency is reached. If necessary, add more water a little at a time to help the consistency of the blend.
4. In a large serving bowl, combine sago pearls, gelatin shapes, blended mango, condensed milk, evaporated milk, and mango chunks. Stir to combine. Serve in individual glasses.

Slow Cooker Hot Chocolate

Want a recipe so effortless but also so crowd-pleasing that your guests will be raving about it afterward? Cue Slow Cooker Hot Chocolate! This creamy delight is more than just hot chocolate; it's coziness in a pot and will make your holiday party even more memorable. Just set up a hot cocoa bar with a slow cooker, marshmallows, candy canes, and all things sweater weather, and watch everyone make their own custom mug!

SERVES 10

2 (4-ounce) bars semisweet baking chocolate, chopped

2 (4-ounce) bars milk baking chocolate, chopped

2 teaspoons vanilla extract (or 1 vanilla bean)

6 cups whole milk

2½ cups heavy cream

2 (12-ounce) cans evaporated milk

1. Add all ingredients to a slow cooker. Cook on low 2 hours, stirring occasionally to ensure mixture doesn't burn.
2. When ready to serve, ladle into mugs. Enjoy!

#ForYou Tips

For a richer cocoa taste, add more of the semisweet chocolate and less of the milk chocolate. You can also add mini marshmallows to the slow cooker right before serving.

Glow in the Dark Drink

Not much is as worthy of going viral as a drink that can glow in the dark, and this is one you won't wanna miss. The secret is the tonic water, which makes it glow under black light. This drink not only tastes good but is the perfect throwback to basement raves. Just bring out the glow sticks and fun music and you'll be enjoying this drink with your friends for hours.

SERVES 6

6 ounces blue curaçao
6 ounces vodka
18 ounces purple energy drink
18 ounces Sprite soda
18 ounces tonic water

1. Fill six clear glasses with ice. Carefully add 1 ounce blue curaçao to each. Then top each glass with 1 ounce vodka, 3 ounces energy drink, and 3 ounces Sprite and mix.
2. Carefully add 3 ounces tonic water to each glass, reveal under black light, then serve.

#ForYou Tips

Make things even more fun by serving these up in unique-looking glasses.

Santa Jell-O Hats

Christmas just got even more festive with these Santa Jell-O shots. And they aren't just cute; they are oh so sweet! These bursts of fruity goodness are not only addictive but perfect for your next holiday party.

SERVES 12

2 (0.25-ounce) packets unflavored gelatin

1 (3-ounce) packet strawberry-flavored gelatin mix

1 cup vodka

¼ cup heavy whipping cream

1 tablespoon confectioners' sugar

12 fresh strawberries, green tops cut off

1. Place unflavored gelatin and 2 tablespoons water in a small bowl and whisk. Set aside 5 minutes until gelatin absorbs all water.
2. Place strawberry gelatin mix in a medium bowl and add 1 cup boiling water. Whisk until combined. Add bloomed unflavored gelatin and whisk again. Set aside to cool at room temperature 5–10 minutes (only enough that it's still liquid). Stir in vodka.
3. Fill twelve 2.5-ounce plastic cups ¾ full with gelatin mixture. Refrigerate uncovered overnight to set, at least 8 hours.
4. In a medium bowl, beat cream and sugar.
5. Remove cups from refrigerator and place on a platter. Using a bag fitted with a piping tip, pipe about ½ tablespoon whipped cream onto each shot and top with 1 strawberry, cut side down. Pipe a small whipped cream pom-pom on the tip of each strawberry. Refrigerate until right before serving, up to 2 days.

Grinch Mimosa

These Grinch Mimosas are yummy, green with a little grinchy envy, and perfect for holiday gatherings. The novelty is in the way these are served—with sparkling green glitter! Watching its color change from blue to green as you pour in the cocktail's signature orange juice is mesmerizing; it's no wonder it's trending! With sweet and bubbly flavors, the Grinch Mimosa will really make your parties extra special 🥰

SERVES 6

3 teaspoons red edible glitter
3 ounces blue curaçao
24 ounces prosecco
18 ounces orange juice
3 teaspoons green edible glitter
6 fresh strawberry slices, cut into heart shapes

1. Wet the rims of 6 champagne flutes with water and dip in red glitter.
2. In each champagne flute, add ½ ounce blue curaçao, 4 ounces prosecco, and 3 ounces orange juice. Stir in ½ teaspoon green glitter. Repeat with remaining rimmed glasses.
3. Garnish each with a strawberry heart and enjoy!

#ForYou Tips

🔥 **To make this drink extra festive, you can pour the orange juice into food-safe ornaments and serve the champagne flutes with the ornaments on top, so guests can pour the orange juice themselves and watch the color change from blue to green.**

Holiday Sangria

Sangria is making a comeback—it's the best way to earn an A on your hosting scorecard. This season, you *won't* be able to resist Holiday Sangria! Its cozy blend of sweet, crisp, fruity flavors will be the talk of any gathering.

SERVES 8

1 cup apple cider
⅓ cup cranberry juice
½ cup vodka
1 (750 mL) bottle dry white wine
¾ cup Cointreau
2 medium oranges, sliced, plus more for garnish
2 medium honeycrisp apples, sliced, plus more for garnish
5 cinnamon sticks
5–6 sprigs fresh rosemary
1 cup ginger beer
1 (750 mL) bottle prosecco

1. In a large pitcher, add apple cider, cranberry juice, vodka, wine, and Cointreau. Stir well.
2. Gently layer orange and apple slices on top. Add cinnamon sticks and rosemary sprigs. Refrigerate until ready to serve, up to 1 day.
3. To serve, carefully add in ginger beer and prosecco, stir, and then pour into eight white wine glasses. Optional: For an extra chill, you can also serve over ice.

Cotton Candy Shots

Who would wanna miss out on the bliss of Cotton Candy Shots?! With its smooth, cool, creamy texture, yet sweet taste, you (and your guests) will be convinced this one comes right out of a candy shop. Pour your shots, watch the cotton candy melt within seconds, and enjoy!

SERVES 6–8

½ cup vanilla ice cream

3 teaspoons cotton candy extract

6 ounces cotton candy–flavored vodka

6 ounces vanilla-flavored vodka

2 drops pink food coloring

Corn syrup

Pink and blue sprinkles

1 (1-ounce) tub pink cotton candy

1 (1-ounce) tub blue cotton candy

1. In a blender, add ice cream, cotton candy extract, cotton candy vodka, and vanilla vodka. Blend until fully smooth. Add food coloring.
2. Rim six 2.5-ounce shot glasses with corn syrup, then add pink and blue sprinkles. Pour blended mixture into glasses and top with either blue or pink cotton candy.

Froot Loops Shots

Froot Loops Shots let you eat your cereal and then drink it too! A creative way to add childhood nostalgia to adult life, this viral shot made with Froot Loops–flavored vodka is definitely gonna be a hit at your next party.

SERVES 6

¼ cup Three Olives Loopy vodka
⅓ cup half-and-half
3 tablespoons blue curaçao
Froot Loops cereal

1. In a large cocktail shaker filled with ice, add vodka, half-and-half, and blue curaçao. Cover and shake 2–3 minutes until chilled.
2. Pour mixture into six 2.5-ounce shot glasses.
3. Top each shot with 5–6 Froot Loops. Make sure to include all different colors on each shot.

CHAPTER 7

Mocktails & Cocktails

Sleepy Girl Mocktail

Mocktails are back in, and this one is especially popular for anyone who's ready for the best night's sleep. This viral concoction comes together to improve your sleep with all its natural melatonin and calming ingredients. Goodbye, wine o'clock, hello, Sleepy Girl Mocktail!

SERVES 1

½ cup tart cherry juice
1 tablespoon magnesium powder
4–6 ice cubes
¼ cup lemon-lime sparkling water or seltzer
1 lime wheel
1 sprig rosemary

1. In a tall glass, add cherry juice and magnesium powder and stir until dissolved.
2. Add ice cubes, then top with sparkling water or seltzer. Garish with lime wheel and rosemary and enjoy!

#ForYou Tips

For an even more well-rested night, try to use low- or no-sugar sparkling water, as higher sugar content can affect the quality of your sleep!

Adrenal Mocktail

Everyone's goal is less stress, and for the thirsty folks, why not have a drink that will boost your immune system *and* become your new wake-up coffee replacement? Loaded with lots of vitamin C and potassium, this drink has citrus flavors with a hint of coconut 🤤 Viral because of its energy-boosting properties, the Adrenal Mocktail is the perfect morning sipper!!!

SERVES 1

1 medium orange, juiced, plus 2 orange slices for garnish

½ cup coconut water

⅛ teaspoon sea salt

¼ teaspoon cream of tartar

2 tablespoons solids from canned coconut cream

1. In a cocktail shaker filled with ice, add ¼ cup orange juice, coconut water, salt, cream of tartar, and solids from coconut cream. Shake 2–3 minutes until chilled.
2. Fill a 16-ounce Mason jar mug with ice. Place orange slices inside mug so they're touching the sides. Pour in orange juice mixture. Enjoy!

Negroni Spritz

The Negroni Spritz went viral because of its lighter take on the classic Negroni. The Negroni *and* this bubbly twist are being made in the luxe homes of many celebs across the world. And now you can sip the lavish lifestyle too!

SERVES 1

1 ounce Campari
1 ounce gin
1 ounce vermouth
4 ounces prosecco
1 orange slice

In a medium glass filled with ice, add Campari, gin, vermouth, and prosecco. Top with orange slice and enjoy!

Blood Orange Wine Spritz

The refreshing taste and bubbly elegance will be the highlight of your summer.

SERVES 1

½ cup blood orange juice
2 tablespoons Aperol
½ cup white wine of choice or prosecco
¼ cup carbonated water
1–2 blood oranges slices

1. In a large wine glass filled with ice, add blood orange juice and Aperol.
2. Carefully pour wine or prosecco and carbonated water over top.
3. Add blood orange slices for garnish and enjoy!

Summer Sunrise Mocktail

The Summer Sunrise Mocktail is sweet meets sparkling with a cherry twist. It has your classic Shirley Temple, orange, pomegranate, and bubbly vibes all in one place!!! 😋

SERVES 1

2 tablespoons grenadine
¾ cup orange juice
½ cup Sprite soda
1 orange wedge
3 maraschino cherries

1. In a tall glass or champagne flute, slowly pour in grenadine. Then add orange juice and Sprite.
2. Garnish with an orange wedge and maraschino cherries. Enjoy!

Spiked Dirty Shirley

Childhood is having a comeback! With a refreshing lime twist and that grenadine sweetness, #DrinkTok knows that Spiked Dirty Shirleys are where it's at.

SERVES 1

1 ounce vodka
1 ounce triple sec
½ ounce lime juice
1 ounce grenadine
4 ounces Sprite soda
3 maraschino cherries

Add ice to a tall glass and pour in vodka, triple sec, lime juice, and grenadine. Top with Sprite and garnish with maraschino cherries skewered on a cocktail pick.

Aperol Spritz

The Aperol Spritz has been going viral due to its lower alcohol content and also its wildly refreshing, bubbly taste. If you're not a fan of the sweet drinks, then this might just be your vibe. Originating in Italy, the Aperol Spritz combines orange bitters with prosecco. Together, you get a delicious—and superclass—cocktail.

SERVES 1

2 ounces Aperol
3 ounces prosecco
1 ounce club soda
1 orange wheel

1. Fill a large wine glass with ice.
2. Pour in Aperol, then add prosecco.
3. Top with club soda and garnish with an orange wheel.

#ForYou Tips

Don't have an ounce measurement? No problem! You can use your fingers to measure the ingredients: Just put your hand around the glass and pour 2 fingers Aperol, 3 fingers prosecco, and 1 finger club soda.

Corona Sunrise

Move aside, tequila sunrise, it's the Corona Sunrise's time to shine! This classic cocktail spin-off is made more fun and tasty with those relaxing beer-by-the-beach vibes. The Corona Sunrise went viral when it was made right in the beer bottle. And the best part? You can bring it to a gathering or enjoy it solo.

SERVES 1

1 (12-ounce) bottle Corona beer
2 ounces tequila
3 ounces orange juice
½ ounce grenadine
1 lime wedge

1. Pour out ¼ cup Corona from bottle.
2. Add tequila, orange juice, and grenadine to bottle. Place lime wedge on top of the bottle.
3. To mix, carefully push lime wedge into the bottle, hold your thumb over top of the bottle to avoid spillage, and flip the bottle upside down. Wait to see lime wedge move to the bottom of the bottle, mixing all ingredients. Flip upright and enjoy!

Corona
Extra
SINCE 1925
LA CERVEZA MAS FINA
IMPORTED
BEER
Brewed and Bottled by
CERVECERIA MODELO
MEXICO
12 FL. OZ.

Mimosa Mom Hack

Let's face it, you aren't always in the mood for a warm beverage in the morning, and ice can just make a whole drink taste watered down. So the moms of TikTok shared this mimosa hack, and it has been taking over social media ever since. The trick is freezing orange juice as the ice, so as it melts, you get *more* flavor. It's the tastiest match for poolside and classy brunches.

SERVES 2

6 thin orange slices

1 cup orange juice, plus more for ice tray

1 cup champagne or prosecco

1. Carefully roll orange slices to make a flower shape. Place one in each section of a large-cube ice tray and pour orange juice to fill. Freeze at least 4 hours until solid.
2. In two short glasses, add orange juice ice cubes.
3. Pour ½ cup orange juice in each glass and top each with ½ cup champagne or prosecco.

#ForYou Tips

Try different fruits and juices like pineapple, mango, or cranberry for different types of mimosas.

Raspberry Lime Mojito

It's not just classic mojitos hitting the viral spotlight; the variations are coming in *hard*, and this Raspberry Lime Mojito is no exception. This combo of minty light flavor is 🔥 It's perfect for a relaxing evening or as a cooldown on a hot day!!!

SERVES 1

3–4 fresh raspberries
1–2 lime wedges
1 tablespoon granulated sugar (or 1 ounce simple syrup)
6 fresh mint leaves
1 ounce white rum
½ cup carbonated water

1. In a medium glass, add raspberries, lime, sugar, and mint. Muddle into a paste that is fully juiced.
2. In a 15-ounce glass with a little ice, strain in muddled juices, leaving out lime wedges and any unnecessary pulp. Add rum and stir to mix.
3. Top off with carbonated water, stir once more, and enjoy.

Pickle Martini

There's no denying that pickles are having their moment online, and why shouldn't they? They're sour, salty, crunchy, and have somewhat of a choke hold on us, which is why the Pickle Martini is going viral! This super simple classic is the perfect way to handle that pickle craving while also enjoying a refreshing and elegant drink with the crew. This version is nonalcoholic because everyone should be able to enjoy a classy martini when they're feeling it!

SERVES 1

1 ounce pickle juice, chilled
2 ounces sparkling water, chilled
1 small gherkin

1. In a martini glass, add pickle juice and sparkling water.
2. To garnish, skewer gherkin and carefully place on top of glass.

#ForYou Tips

Turn this martini into an adults-only moment by adding 2 ounces chilled vodka.

Cotton Candy Margarita

Nothing beats the carnival vibes of cotton candy—especially when you can have it in your own home! This Cotton Candy Margarita brings those nostalgic childhood feels back, and why *shouldn't* you enjoy a sentimental drink? This recipe has been catching waves online because of its mesmerizing dissolution of the cotton candy in the glass.

SERVES 2

2 tablespoons coarse salt
1½ medium limes, divided
4 ounces tequila
2 ounces triple sec
1 (1-ounce) tub cotton candy
1 (12-ounce) can cream soda

1. Pour salt onto a small plate. Juice 1 lime—you should have 2 tablespoons lime juice. From remaining ½ lime, cut two lime wheels, then cut remainder into two wedges.
2. Rub a lime wedge around the rim of a margarita glass and press rim into salt. Repeat with second glass and remaining lime wedge.
3. In a cocktail shaker filled with ice, add tequila, triple sec, 2 tablespoons lime juice, and ¾ cup cotton candy. Shake 2–3 minutes until chilled.
4. Pour into prepared glasses and top with cream soda. Carefully place a chunk of cotton candy over each glass and garnish with lime wheels. Serve and enjoy.

#ForYou Tips

If you're not a fan of the lime and salt rim, you can swap for corn syrup and small pink sprinkles.

Long Island Iced Tea

They say the Long Island Iced Tea is delicious but deadly. This concoction of alcohol is no joke, but it's also full of delicious flavor! Everything in this trendy classic works together to create the most beautiful lemony-tasting drink.

SERVES 1

1 ounce Coke soda
½ ounce vodka
½ ounce white rum
½ ounce gin
½ ounce triple sec
½ ounce tequila
½ ounce lemon juice
1 ounce simple syrup
1 lemon wedge

1. In a cocktail shaker filled with ice, add all ingredients except lemon wedge. Shake 1–2 minutes until thoroughly mixed.
2. In a tall glass, add ice to fill. Pour in mixture. Top with a lemon wedge and a straw. Enjoy!

Piña Colada Mocktail

If you like piña coladas, you'll looove this irresistible mocktail Pineapples are kind of the GOAT of fruit right now, and people have been making them into all kinds of desserts and drinks. With all the same classic pineapple, coconut flavors, this creamy drink screams vacation vibes!!!

SERVES 1

1 cup frozen pineapple chunks
½ cup canned coconut cream
¼ cup pineapple juice
1 pineapple wedge
1 maraschino cherry

1. In a blender, add pineapple chunks, coconut cream, and pineapple juice and blend until it all reaches a smoothie texture. Add more pineapple juice if needed.
2. Pour into a hurricane glass, top with pineapple wedge and cherry, and enjoy.

#ForYou Tips

Like a slushier texture? Add some ice to the blender!

Lemon Moscow Mule

Moscow mules are that wonderfully underrated gem everyone is finally talking about. With a signature copper cup, it's one of those drinks that feels fancy but is so wonderfully easy to make. So refreshing with ginger beer, lemon, and mint flavors, it'll earn a spot on your weeknight go-to list.

SERVES 1

¼ cup vodka
2 tablespoons lemon juice
1 tablespoon simple syrup
½ cup ginger beer
1 lemon wheel
1 sprig fresh mint

1. Fill a copper mug with ice. Stir in vodka, lemon juice, and simple syrup.
2. Pour ginger beer over top and garnish with lemon wheel and mint sprig. Serve and enjoy!

#ForYou Tips

Mix things up by swapping the lemon with a lime, or even blueberries for a more vibrant summer treat!

Cucumber Mocktail

Move over, cucumber salads because cucumber *drinks* are taking the spotlight! This mocktail pairs the refreshing flavor of cucumber with lime and mint. It's the level up we all needed for hydration!

SERVES 1

1 medium cucumber, divided
3 large fresh mint leaves
2 lime wedges
1 tablespoon honey (or simple syrup)
¾ cup club soda or seltzer
1 sprig fresh mint

1. Cut ½ cucumber into chunks and place in blender. Cut three thin lengthwise strips from the remaining half and set aside. Blend chunks until smooth, then strain 2 ounces cucumber juice into an 8-ounce Mason jar.
2. Add mint leaves and lime wedges to Mason jar. Muddle until lime wedges release their juice and mint is broken down and incorporated. Remove lime wedges and stir in honey.
3. Carefully wrap two cucumber slices around the inside of a tall glass and fill with ice. Pour cucumber mixture into glass. Top with club soda or seltzer and stir well.
4. Thread the remaining cucumber slice onto a skewer and place it on top of the drink. Garnish with mint sprig. Serve and enjoy!

#ForYou Tips

If you're not a fan of mint leaves in your glass, you can pull them out with the lime wedge after you've muddled them.

Lemon Drop

People are going mad for lemon, and the Lemon Drop is definitely worth the hype! This twisted martini is getting its viral moment due to its simple, yet irresistible tangy flavor. With its sour and citrusy essence, it's a delicious gem that'll keep you feeling energized for the night.

SERVES 2

¼ cup granulated sugar

1 medium lemon, zested and cut into wedges

3 ounces vodka

6 ounces lemon juice (from about 4 medium lemons)

1½ ounces triple sec

1½ ounces simple syrup

1. On a plate, add sugar and lemon zest. Mix with a fork until completely combined.
2. Lightly run a lemon wedge around the rims of two martini glasses. Dip rims into lemon sugar and tap lightly until entire rim is coated.
3. In a cocktail shaker filled with ice, add vodka, lemon juice, triple sec, and simple syrup. Shake 2–3 minutes until chilled, then pour evenly into martini glasses. Enjoy!

Lychee Martini

Lychee is the Internet's widespread secret: a sweet red fruit native to China that not everyone knew about before it went viral. And now, lychee has gotten an upgrade thanks to the Lychee Martini. This drink is classy meets elegance; with its light flavor, it's a simple drink that tastes *delicious* 😋

SERVES 1

2 medium lychees, peeled or from a can, plus more for optional garnish

1½ ounces vodka

3 ounces lychee syrup from a can

4 ounces lemon juice (from about 3 medium lemons)

2–3 fresh mint leaves (optional)

1. In a cocktail shaker filled with ice, add all ingredients except mint. Shake 2–3 minutes until chilled and pour into a martini glass.
2. If desired, on a cocktail pick, skewer some lychees and mint and place on top of glass.

Parmesan Espresso Martini

Espresso martinis are having a huge moment online, and this version is especially earning the hype! With the bitter twist of Parmesan in a rich espresso blend, this drink will definitely wake you up. But what's the reason for the odd pairing? A lot of people online say what makes it work is an umami-rich flavoring. It'll become your go-to for celebrating after a long day.

SERVES 1

1 ounce espresso
2 ounces vodka
1 ounce coffee liqueur
1 tablespoon grated Parmesan cheese

1. In a cocktail shaker filled with ice, add espresso, vodka, and coffee liqueur. Shake 2–3 minutes until chilled and pour into a martini glass.
2. Garnish with Parmesan. Enjoy!

Pink Gin Sour

The Pink Gin Sour takes #viral to a whole new level! This drink is frothy and creamy, with the perfect hint of sour flavoring. It's a cocktail worthy of your night off.

SERVES 1

2 ounces pink gin
1 ounce lemon juice
½ ounce simple syrup
1 large egg white
1 teaspoon edible rose petals

In a cocktail shaker filled with ice, add gin, lemon juice, simple syrup, and egg white. Shake 2–3 minutes until chilled. Pour into a cocktail glass and top with rose petals. Enjoy!

Standard US/Metric Measurement Conversions

VOLUME CONVERSIONS	
US Volume Measure	**Metric Equivalent**
⅛ teaspoon	0.5 milliliter
¼ teaspoon	1 milliliter
½ teaspoon	2 milliliters
1 teaspoon	5 milliliters
½ tablespoon	7 milliliters
1 tablespoon (3 teaspoons)	15 milliliters
2 tablespoons (1 fluid ounce)	30 milliliters
¼ cup (4 tablespoons)	60 milliliters
⅓ cup	90 milliliters
½ cup (4 fluid ounces)	125 milliliters
⅔ cup	160 milliliters
¾ cup (6 fluid ounces)	180 milliliters
1 cup (16 tablespoons)	250 milliliters
1 pint (2 cups)	500 milliliters
1 quart (4 cups)	1 liter (about)

WEIGHT CONVERSIONS	
US Weight Measure	**Metric Equivalent**
½ ounce	15 grams
1 ounce	30 grams
2 ounces	60 grams
3 ounces	85 grams
¼ pound (4 ounces)	115 grams
½ pound (8 ounces)	225 grams
¾ pound (12 ounces)	340 grams
1 pound (16 ounces)	454 grams

OVEN TEMPERATURE CONVERSIONS	
Degrees Fahrenheit	**Degrees Celsius**
200 degrees F	95 degrees C
250 degrees F	120 degrees C
275 degrees F	135 degrees C
300 degrees F	150 degrees C
325 degrees F	160 degrees C
350 degrees F	180 degrees C
375 degrees F	190 degrees C
400 degrees F	205 degrees C
425 degrees F	220 degrees C
450 degrees F	230 degrees C

BAKING PAN SIZES	
American	**Metric**
8 × 1½ inch round baking pan	20 × 4 cm cake tin
9 × 1½ inch round baking pan	23 × 3.5 cm cake tin
11 × 7 × 1½ inch baking pan	28 × 18 × 4 cm baking tin
13 × 9 × 2 inch baking pan	30 × 20 × 5 cm baking tin
2 quart rectangular baking dish	30 × 20 × 3 cm baking tin
15 × 10 × 2 inch baking pan	30 × 25 × 2 cm baking tin (Swiss roll tin)
9 inch pie plate	22 × 4 or 23 × 4 cm pie plate
7 or 8 inch springform pan	18 or 20 cm springform or loose bottom cake tin
9 × 5 × 3 inch loaf pan	23 × 13 × 7 cm or 2 lb narrow loaf or pate tin
1½ quart casserole	1.5 liter casserole
2 quart casserole	2 liter casserole

Index

Note: Drink titles with an asterisk* indicate alcohol content.

G

H

I

J

K

L

M

N

P

R

S

T

U

V

W

Author photo by Marc Cartwright Photography

Palestrina McCaffrey, better known as Little Remy Food on social media, is an amateur chef who brings her passion for food and love of learning to the kitchen. With her approachable style and honest feedback, she makes cooking fun and accessible for everyone. Known for testing viral recipes, she has become a trusted resource for home cooks looking to discover which recipes are genuinely worth re-creating. Discover more by following @littleremyfood on your favorite social media platforms.

As seen on #FOODTOK

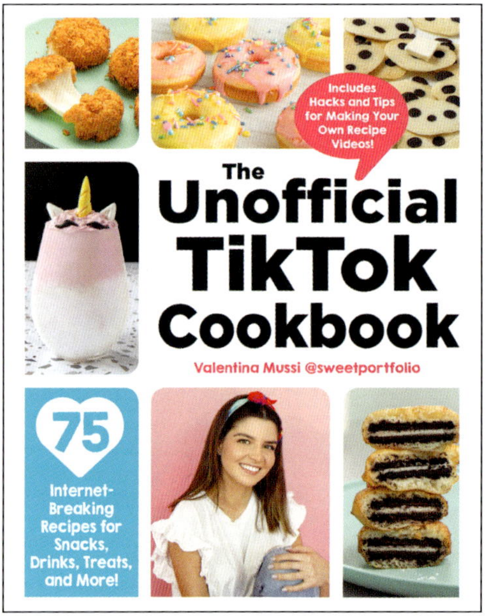

Pick up or download your copies today!

adamsmedia
An Imprint of Simon & Schuster